Print ISBN: 978-0-9860965-1-8
eBook ISBN: 978-0-9860965-0-1

"In My Teenage Dystopian Movie" and "Submissions Editor at Dreams
Quarterly" first appeared in newyorker.com.
"The Brooklyn Invitational Nobel Prize for Literature Fantasy League
Draft" originally appeared in the *Barnes & Noble Review* on October 8, 2014.

Cover photo by Michael T. Kaufman

This is a work of fiction. Names, characters, places and incidents either
are the product of the author's imagination or are used fictitiously. Any
resemblance to actual persons, living or dead, events or locales is entirely
coincidental.

THE WAR AGAINST
BOREDOM
SHORT STORIES, RIFFS & INSANITIES

SETH KAUFMAN

Sukuma
Books

This is for my mom, Rebecca,
with love and gratitude.

TABLE OF DISCONTENTS

IN MY TEENAGE DYSTOPIAN MOVIE

In my teenage dystopian movie aliens attack, and because they have come in search of fake distressed retro-clothing that is inexplicably in short supply on their planet, they capture all the kids who wear Hollister and take them to another galaxy.

At first, me and all the other kids left on earth are like, cool, because does the world really need people who spend large amounts of money shopping in a store that has intentionally bad lighting and intentionally underdressed staff selling intentionally nice but overpriced distressed retro-clothing?

But then it turns out the aliens have left a virus on the earth and it starts killing everyone. It's a horrible virus. First, your voice starts to sound disembodied, like your vocal chords are hooked to autotune. Then your hair and teeth fall out.

When you finally die from the virus, your head explodes. It's like ebola to the tenth power. Which is both horrifying and fantastic to watch, depending on how emotionally invested in my teenage dystopian movie you are.

In my teenage dystopian movie, the virus also kills all vampires and werewolves, which really saddens all the goths and other kids and adults and publishing and movie executives that are into them, but not for very long because they are dying, too.

But then me and my friends Davis, Luke, and Samantha notice that none of the stoner kids are dying. Which is us. And so we figure out that something in pot keeps the virus at bay. So Samantha and I run to her house and bake some pot brownies, fast as we can, which is not that fast, because we are pretty high. But when we're done, we give her family some brownies and explain our theory.

Sam's parents are very cool. Like, the opposite of mine. And when they hear our evidence they gobble the brownies, discuss the awesome, grow-any-where, use-any-in-way power of hemp, and say they are going to call the CDC, if anyone is still alive in Atlanta.

When we get to my house, my father has his Kevlar body-suit on and his machine gun strapped on.

"Reed, what the hell are you doin' going around town?" he says, pointing his gun at me. "You might have the virus."

In my teenage dystopian movie, I explain the situation to my father and of course, he barely listens to me and says, "Are you high, dammit?"

Samantha chimes in. "You have to trust Reed on this, Mr. Winslow."

But instead of trusting me, he tells me that I'm grounded and since I might be an Infected, I will have to live in our doghouse for a while. But it won't be that bad, he tells me, because Rex, his beloved pitbull, will sleep in the house.

"Look, Dad! Aliens in the backyard!" I yell, pointing.

He runs to check and we get the hell out of there.

We pass the house of Kristi Woah, the super hot, super-smart, brainiac who I have had a crush on since she moved to town in ninth grade. When I spot a group of Infecteds outside Kristi's house, I tell Samantha I'll meet her at Tony Strong's. He's our pot dealer who grows hydroponic plants in his basement.

I climb up the ivy vines that lead to Kristi's room. I guess it's hers because there's a big Pi decal on the window and she's in, like, Super-Mega Advanced Quantum AP Math or something. I knock on the glass.

"Why didn't you ring the bell?" she says through the closed window.

"Because there's a group of Infecteds at your front door."

"My parents are medical researchers," she says, opening the window. "Everyone thinks they can help."

"Listen," I say, "There's not much time. We figured out that the virus doesn't work on potheads. I came here to get you stoned."

The doorbell rings. The Infecteds are banging on the door.

"Reed! That is so lame. What is it with you stoners? Anything to get high."

"No, no. Kristi. I swear. Samantha and I just gave her family pot brownies to help them survive." Then I explain our reasoning and give her all the names of the Infecteds at school.

"Your empirical evidence is impressive, Reed. Okay. I'll try it."

I fire up a bowl and pass it to her. She takes a tiny, tentative toke and coughs her head off, spewing out the smoke. "I can't do it."

There is banging at the door. The Infecteds are going to bust in.

"Here, Kristi," I say, in my teenage dystopian movie, "Until you get the hang of it, there's only one other way. Tomorrow, we can bake brownies for you, but for now, this will just take a second—"

We can hear the door crash open. The Infecteds are screaming in their horrible autotune-on-ten voices, which sound like Maroon Five being played at supersonic speed. I fire up the bowl and gather a cloud of smoke in my cheeks. Then I press my lips against Kristi's and say, "Mmpn mr mwf!"

Her lips open and I blow the smoke into her mouth in a steady stream, shotgun style. And when the I'm done, I pull away, which is like the hardest thing to do in the entire world. But I have to, because there's the clomping sound of someone coming up the steps. I rush to the landing and kick a lumbering Infected in the chest, sending him back down the stairs.

"Come on," I say, grabbing Kristi's hand and lifting her to her feet.

"We've got to get to Tony Strong's house and protect his stash!"

But Kristi's a little red-eyed and smiley now. She looks at me, laughs, and says, "Reed, what was *that?*"

"Come on," I say, pulling her close, a move that is rewarded with Kristi's red-hot mouth against mine in my teenage dystopian movie, which is now cranking some awesome, ass-kickingly anthemic electro-funk-metal, like Daft Punk sampling Hendrix, on the soundtrack.

When we both come up for air, Kristi's eyes are shining. She says: "Come on. Let's go save the world."

CAFE SHHHH

In my café, Café Shhhh, all the tables have only one chair.

This means there is no loud over-sharing in my cafe. Ever. Remember that guy in some other café describing his new boyfriend? "He's really good looking, and, like, people stop him on the street to tell him that." Or the woman in that tiny Swedish-owned coffee shop who false-complained about how she needed to go shopping for a bathing suit because her husband was taking her to St. Bart's for her birthday? That doesn't happen at Café Shhhh. And that means you will never waste time debating whether or not it is impolite to go over and ask these over-sharers to please talk a little more quietly or even to just go fuck themselves.

The seating policy at Café Shhhh completely eliminates the chance of you sitting down and overhearing first-time parents questioning a prospective nanny about whether she would charge overtime for working 55 hours a week.

And that means you will never have to fight the urge to go up to the parents and say, "Hey, assholes! 55 hours means 15 hours of overtime! Why are you trying to screw this poor woman out of money? Especially when she's taking care of *your baby!*"

In Café Shhhh, you will never have to listen to two people having a "writing session" for their sitcom about a group of misfit friends in New York. And you will never have to stifle the impulse to tell these two that, while you applaud their creative efforts, the chances of this sitcom getting produced range from zero to none. Nor will you have to suppress urge to ask them about the whole "writing partners" thing. Did Mark Twain have a writing partner? Jane Austen? Leo Tolstoy?

In my café, Café Shhhh, you don't need to bring headphones—although you can if you want to—because it's called Café Shhhh and we only play Bach, big band swing and music from Mali at low volumes. The music rarely has vocals sung in English, because songs with lyrics you understand can be really distracting when you are trying to read or write while drinking delicious caffeinated beverages, or even decaffeinated beverages, if that's your thing.

In my café, there is free wi-fi and there is a Café Shhhh web page where people at Café Shhhh can post comments and introduce themselves to other people at the Café. You can post things like, "My name is Jack. I'm sitting next to the Polish circus poster that says Crzk! Today I'm working on the list of cool band names and what the names of their first albums should be. Ping me if you have any suggestions."

You can also post an appropriate response to that post, which might be, "Hi Jack, Band name: Blog My Ass. Album title: *How Not to Get Laid*."

Café Shhhh is the most onomatopoetically named café in the world because Shhhh is the sound of milk being carefully steamed and teakettles hissing. It is also the sound in your mind's ear when you hear someone—at a different café, never, ever at Café Shhhh—talking about their recent painful and expensive visit to a proctologist while you are trying to enjoy a mint tea and a chocolate-chip-oatmeal cookie.

Of course, moments like that may also generate another sound: WTF. But that is a sound rarely heard at Café Shhhh. And if it was heard, there's only one way it would be answered in my café: Shhhh.

ASK ZELDA

An NSA official, writing under the pen name "Zelda," has actually served at the agency as a Dear Abby for spies.

—*The Intercept*

Dear Zelda,

I'm an investigator who, as instructed, has told my girlfriend that I work in "I.T." She likes to play a game called "what if." And the other day she said, "What if you become a spy who has to seduce a secretary at the Soviet embassy who is married to a military attaché there so that she can be blackmailed into obtaining encryption keys for the N.S.A. Would you cheat on me?" I was stunned at first because that is my current assignment. But I played it cool and said that wouldn't be cheating because it was work related. In fact, I'd be a patriot and would probably get a medal. But she got all upset, and insists that cheating is cheating. She hasn't talked to me for a whole week. What should I do?

Signed,
Torn

Dear Agent McKinsey,

Now that I've discussed your case internally at the highest levels of the Agency, I must advise you not to become too emotionally attached to this young woman. Our friends at The Company are looking into finding Nancy a new job in a new town where she can find a new boyfriend.

Dear Zelda,

Some of my staffers think it would be hilarious to do a version of a song called "Renditionally" for the big Christmas party. It's a parody of Katy Perry's hit song, "Unconditionally." I think this is in really bad taste, plus, if it leaks onto the web, we'll be seen as making fun of torture. Should I pull rank and tell them this is not appropriate?

Signed,
Rock and Hard Place

Dear Ms. Leslie,

Cancel the performance, and you are being a power-tripping, censorious paper-pusher. Let it go on, and you risk losing your job and having your whole division shut down. Both are clear and present dangers. Therefore, invent a budgetary crisis and cancel the Christmas party. Problem solved.

Dear Zelda,

My wife thinks her brother-in-law "Bob," who has a green card, is cheating on her sister, Melissa. She wants me to hack Bob's email and texts so she can open Melissa's eyes. I say spying on a foreigner is one thing, but spying on your family is a gross abuse of power. What do you say?

Signed,
Brother-in-Arms

Dear Descrambler Evans,

Is Bob an American? No. Plus, he married into the family, so he's not a blood relative to either you or your wife. Some might consider him a "double foreigner" in this regard. Here at the NSA we are okay with whistleblowing on domestic matters of the heart, especially if it reduces friction with the missus. Spy with a clean conscience.

Dear Zelda,

I'm a senior manager with the Cryptanalysis team. We were playing softball against the guys in Computer Engineering, who kept holding up their middle, index and ring fingers and yelling, "Hey Analysts, read between the lines!" It was annoying and distracting and they beat us 8 to 3. Now my team is working with the guys at Installation & Logistics to install a program so that an image of "the finger" will pop up whenever Computer Engineering guys log on. Should I stop this or let the revenge continue?

Signed,
XcT256709BBVv098

Dear Sr. Manager Johnson,

This is a real team building project, which is great for morale. Go ahead with the prank, and make this a teachable moment, too. Leave a message below the obscene graphic. Something like: "Looking forward to your improved sportsmanship next year, suckers."

Dear Zelda,

A number of my staff here in India work under deep cover for NGO's without diplomatic status. These employees were recently banned from using the American Club, no thanks to tit-for-tat posturing after the U.S. bounced a Delhi diplomat stationed in New York. Now my guys are asking for false documents that list them as embassy personnel, and I just can't make that happen. They are claiming hardship and accuse the Agency of a two-tiered caste system. Any suggestions to quash this uprising?

Desperate in Delhi

Dear Chief of Station Goldman,

It is always tough to lose a perk, but try putting it in perspective for your rabble-rousers. The next time they complain, ask if they are happy with the chef who cooks their meals, the sweeper who cleans their houses, and the dhoti who does their laundry. Also ask if they love being able to take weekend trips to the Taj Mahal or Rajasthan as much as you do. Then ask if they would like a transfer to Damascus, Caracas or Sana, because you can make that happen. Problem solved.

CAN YOU HANDLE
A SEX SCANDAL?

Take our quiz to see if you've got what it takes to be a master of disaster.

1. Are you famous, almost famous, rich, or actually very talented?
    a. Yes (5 pts)
    b. No (2 pts)

2. Are any of your family and friends famous, almost famous, rich or actually very talented?
    a. Yes (5 pts)
    b. No (2 pts)

3. Do you consider Kardashian an adjective?
    a. Yes (2 pts)
    b. No (5 pts)
    c. Don't understand the question (10 pts)

4. Can your name or profession be linked to a popular song, TV show or movie title in a way that has sexual overtones? Think hard. Everything has sexual overtones, including the statement "Think hard."

    a. Yes (10 pts)

    b. No (5 pts)

5. Which of the following terms best describes your attitudes toward hook ups?

    a. YOLO (10 pts)

    b. OTDL (10 pts)

    c. Swag! (10 pts)

    d. I have a DSL connection (0 pts)

6. How good are you at lying?

    a. Not very. (1 pt)

    b. Deny, deny, deny. (5 pts)

    c. It depends on what the meaning of the word 'lying' is. (8 pts)

    d. Hey! You'll never guess what happened to me today! (10 pts)

7. Which statement best describes your relationship with your cellphone?

    a. It's complicated. (5 pts)

    b. Hold on a sec, let me just finish this text. (10 pts)

    c. I can't figure out how to check messages. (2 pts)

    d. I could hack the Pentagon but I'm so paranoid about NSA surveillance, I've gone off the grid. (0 pts)

8. Are you a clergy member, athlete, politician or cop?

    a. Yes (10 pts)

    b. No (2 pts)

    c. No comment (10 pts)

9. When someone mentions sexting, you:
   a. Confuse the term with sextet. (2 pts)
   b. Reach for your phone. (5 pts)
   c. Just don't understand. (2 pts)
   d. Wonder about those pix from three years ago. (10 pts)

10. Which nom de nookie (that's French for "scandal handle") would you choose for yourself?
   a. Naughty'n'NextDoor (4 pts)
   b. TheLonelyUnicorn (1 pt)
   c. YoI'mTheWad (5 pts)
   d. BarelyLegal (10 pts)

11. Do you know how to send a private message on Twitter?
   a. Yes (5 pts)
   b. No (5 pts)

12. When it comes to justifying your actions, you:
   a. Can justify anything. (10 pts)
   b. Accept full responsibility. (2 pts)
   c. Accept full responsibility but none of the blame. (10 pts)
   d. Are really sorry and thank everyone for understanding this personal matter. (10pts)

Your Score

Under 30: ScanDEAD. Your mojo is MIA. When it comes to subterfuge, deviance, polymorphous perversity and scuzzy behavior, you are flatlining.

Under 30-50: ScanDULL. Your game needs serious work. Start small: More Bravo, less PBS. More porn, less PTA.

Then post a profile on J-Date or Christian Mingle.

51-to-75: ScanDAMN! *Ooh-la-la!* (That's French for "ooh-la-la.") You've got the goods, but do you have guile?

Over 75: ScanDALICIOUS! You are a danger to yourself and everyone you are sleeping with, or want to sleep with. Make sure you have a publicist, an agent, a lawyer and some loyal friends. Oh, and a really good headshot.

BAGS THAT COULD
SAVE THE WORLD

Still, nothing the company ever did hit the jackpot like Mr. Murakami's cherry-ornamented and "Multico" bags, which came about, as Mr. Carcelle explained, after 9/11, when the Vuitton designer, Marc Jacobs, suggested to his corporate bosses that it was no good to mourn forever: fashion had a responsibility, ahem, to help people past their grief. "Marc said," Mr. Carcelle recalled, "'If I work with Takashi, and we do something colorful, I think it will help make New York strong again.'"

    —*New York Times,* Sunday Style Section, April 6, 2008

Dear Yves and Takashi, here are some new ideas. Let me know what you think.

    The Barrage Bag: Remember when London defended itself from the blitz by hoisting huge balloons over notable buildings—like Seville Row, Harrods, Paul Smith, and, some palaces? Same idea here, but bigger and baggier. Here's what I'm thinking: 10 massive inflatable bubble purses with

4 ginormous outside pockets, each with their own gilded clasps engraved with very subtle *LV*'s. Can you imagine the light hitting them? OMG. I'm breathless. Materials? We can just use whatever the Goodyear blimp uses. It's not like Tim Gunn is going to fly up in a helicopter and touch them to find out, right? Set up a meeting with the mayor to discuss this new addition to the skyline.

The Khyber Croc Clutch: Approach Pentagon and State Department with foolproof peace plan. The hook? 10,000 gorgeous croc clutches. We airdrop all of them—with darling linen parachutes. Can you imagine the photo op? I can hear you saying I've lost my mind. Well, just consider this: When those poor, oppressed women and their jihadi hubbies feel genuine crocodile skin, they will go out of their minds and understand the ways of the West. It will be like the hajj to the 10th power. And let me tell you, the Taliban are going to have a hard time shooting their AK-47s when they can't bear to let go of the ultimate bag. Note: if government balks at price, suggest dropping knock-offs.

The O-Bag, or Glad Sack: How can the first truly luxe condom save the world? Bear with me—and, no, this wasn't what I was thinking of when I first started designing bags. The power of the O-Bag—scented, flavored latex—lies less in design than in marketing. With the right price-point ($100 for a box of 10?) and a tag line *(Even better than sex!),* the O-Bag will erase the condom's "taking-a-bath-in-a-raincoat" stigma and become the most popular safe sex device since the invention of marriage. Everyone will want them because, newsflash: status equals sex. Do I hear the words Nobel Prize?

Kobe Saddlebags: You know how people say things about our line like, "I would kill for that bag"? Well the idea here is to make a bag so great, you have to *stop* killing to get it. I'm thinking of the ultimate bag here, exclusively made to stop the madness in Darfur. Black Wagyu cattle leather saddlebags adorned with cowrie shells, pearls and gold, perfect for camels, bikes, motorcycles. Strong, yet oh-so-supple, these bags would be distributed as part of a peace deal. Let's get Kofi's replacement, Bain de Soleil, and see if we can't put something together.

My cell is ringing. Probably Oslo calling. Gotta go.

Marc

SONG OF MY SELFIES

It is not easy to be a completely self-involved artist. People are always asking for studio visits, proposals, dinner dates and interviews. It 's a constant struggle, what with my work, and my FB, Twitter, Instagram, Tumblr, Google+, Pintrest and Snapchat updates, not to mention my blog and my posts on Renren and Orkut for foreign dealers and fans. I worry that I'm getting distracted. The other day I caught myself wondering if my gorgeous studio assistant might be bored watching me be self-involved. Is that the kind of question a true self-involved artist asks? No! And so I decided to combat these demons with the most self-involved project in the history of self-involvement. Here's a preview:

"Say Uncle" Nov. 2013

Oh, man. This was great! My four-year-old niece Matilda was posing with some guy dressed as Elmo in the middle of Times Square. Matty was completely thrilled! And my sister-in-law was yelling, "Take the picture! Take the picture!" So, boom! Here it is. Things got a little ugly later on when

Elmo asked me for $5 bucks, and I tried to explain on the QT that, although it looked like I was taking his picture, I actually took a selfie of the moment that I was supposed to be taking the picture of Matty and him together—which of course is a photographic study in self-reflexivity and the denial of the other. Then Elmo said, in a very un-Elmo-like voice: "You want me to fuck you up, man?" which is the kind of question that instantly cuts to the core of self-involvement. The answer was an unequivocal no and I paid him $5. When Matilda asked to see the picture, I got on my knees to her level (so her mom couldn't hear) and explained that the camera broke and that the joyful experience of meeting Elmo was much more important than an actual picture. Then we went to the M&M store and I bought her a giant bag of red M&Ms—is there any other color?—that she will never forget and my sister-in-law will never forgive.

"Is the Flash On?" Nov. 2013

Here I am with Maggie from Nashville after barbeque and bourbon at Virgil's. I'll never forget how she posed this shot. She said, "Hey! Take a picture of me right when the #1 train pulls in and I'll flash ya!" She has a really great smile and wind from the train blew her messy auburn hair in front of her face as she lifted her shirt up and exposed her alabaster and crimson breasts, which are outstanding. I was a little nervous about missing the moment. Fortunately, I just nailed it. Whew!

"I'm Not with The Band" Dec. 2013

Outside Le Poisson Rouge on Bleecker St. my pals Monroe and Alice insisted on posing with guys from the band we saw. But the musicians, acting cooler than Freon®, wouldn't crack a smile. I said, "Come on, guys! This is rock and roll. Do I have to be a court jester here?" Click! Obviously, I did the work for them. Alice, who has a face that could launch 2000 ships, was wearing a really unflattering dress and Monroe had grown an unfortunate mustache. So I think this photo really does everyone a favor.

"Journey to the Center of His Mind" Dec. 2013

As you can see, I'm not entirely comfortable pretending to take pictures of strangers on trains. You never know how the ignored subject is going to act about you seeming to take his or her picture, even though you are not, in fact, taking his or her picture. In this case the stranger was a young man who was so busy ranting to the entire subway car about not getting a job that he didn't seem to mind. "They tell you to dress up, and you *still* don't get the job. What am I supposed to do? Paint myself gold? Silver? I'm allergic to silver!" It was the most memorable rant in all my years of riding the subway. I wish you had been there.

"My Brother's Keeper" January, 2014

Me, my broken nose, and I in the ER. Remember my Times Square picture? A few weeks later, my brother, who does not really appreciate my art the way my 104,011 Twitter followers, my 350,026 FB friends and everyone at my gallery does, asked me for the picture of Matty with Elmo. When I explained my recent project, he hauled off and clocked me. Then, apologizing profusely, he took me to the ER. After the doc reset my nose, my brother demanded I take a selfie of the two of us. I said, "How is that a selfie?" And he said, "Just do it." So I did. Then I airbrushed him the hell out of the picture. Gotta love Photoshop.

THE MALTESE CUPCAKE

In an effort to limit how much sugar and fat students put in their bellies at school, the Education Department has effectively banned most bake sales, the lucrative if not quite healthy fund-raising tool for generations of teams and clubs.

—*NY Times*, Oct. 2. 2009

Effie instant messaged Sam Spade from the front office. There was woman outside who wanted to talk to him. Spade finished rolling the cigarette that he would have to go downstairs to actually smoke, checked his camera setup, and then IM'd Effie to send her in.

As soon as his door opened, Spade clicked his mouse, snapping a picture of his prospective client. Then he remembered to close his jaw, which had dropped.

The woman in front of him had better curves than a Grand Prix racetrack trapped in a Mobius strip. She was a strawberry blonde, tall, dressed to accentuate the positive. The kind of girl who spelled danger, except that wherever she went, nobody would be interested in spelling.

"Mr. Spade," she said, taking a seat. "I'm so glad you could see me. I'm very afraid I, I mean, my...sister is in trouble."

"Trouble265 is my Twitter name," Spade said. "Ms....?"

"Wolf. Helen Wolf. It's not me I'm here about. My older sister, Marie, she's...oh, we're all so worried."

The bombshell started weeping. This always happened. The sap play. Spade pushed a box of tissues across the desk.

"Why don't you start from the beginning, Ms. Wolf?" Spade said.

"It all started with the Bake Sale ban. That dreadful Department of Education." Spade watched as Ms. Wolf gave a little shiver. He was a detective, so he noticed her bosom shiver too.

"Marie was just starting to find her stride. After the school auction was such a success, she started planning the mother of all bake sales. They had donations from everywhere: the Cupcake Café, Magnolia Bakery, and the Food Network and CNN were going to cover it. One of the parents was developing an app for the event so you could place orders from your smartphone."

"Sounds impressive," said Spade.

"Yes. Not only that, she was going to unveil her own masterpiece, The Cupcake Club—a double decker devil's food cupcake with two layers of icing, one in the middle and one on top. Then she vanished."

"Vanished?" Spade said.

"Yesterday she called me and said she met a custodian who believed in the cause. He said he had access to secret room in the school. And if they kept it on the QT, they could pull off the sale of the century. Even with the ban."

"Where's her husband? Where does he figure in this?"

"Blake? He would never allow this. He voted for Bloomberg. Three times."

"Any problems in the marriage?"

"Just the normal ones."

Spade fought off a smile. He'd heard an earful about normal problems from his partner Archer's wife.

"I'm not sure this is my kind of case, Ms. Wolf."

She opened her handbag, reached in and produced a wad of $100 bills. "I'm sure this will cover any expenses."

Spade nodded. "My partner Archer will case the school tonight. That's P.S....?"

"P.S. 87," said Helen Wolf, looking anxious. "Do you think you can find her?"

"We'll do our best. Leave your info and your deposit with Effie."

Spade rolled out of bed and answered his cellphone. It was 3 a.m. He figured it would be a distraught Helen Wolf.

"Yeah," he croaked.

"Sorry, Spade." It was Leary from Homicide. "You better come down here. The school on West 78th Street."

Spade wrote down the address and took a cab. Archer was a mess. His face was an orgy of oozing chocolate frosting, cake crumbs, sprinkles and blood. Spade was disgusted. "Any leads?"

"Just a box from Inter-Continental Chocolates," said Leary. "Blackout Chocolate Cupcakes. What was he doing here?"

"Casing the joint. Looking for an AWOL PTA mom."

"A bake sale biddy?"

"Whaddya mean?" Spade said. This was rule #1: always

play dumb with the cops.

"The intelligence unit says there's a whole underground movement. The mayor would never stand a chance at re-election after that bake sale ban. I mean, Christ, no bake sales?"

Spade nodded. He said, "Elementary school. Not something I follow." Then he sighed. "I better go tell Archer's wife."

There was a fat man in the office when Spade made it to work around noon the next day. The man was sitting and sweating. He looked uncomfortable in his own skin.

"Sam," Effie said, "this is Mr. Jim Continental."

"Continental, huh?" Spade said. "Why don't you come in to my office?"

The fat man started talking as soon has he stepped into Spade's office.

"It's my real name. Continental. Of Inter-Continental Chocolates—Manhattan, Brooklyn, Queens."

"Okay, Mr. Continental, what's on your mind?"

"I invested in a project, developing a new chocolate. A new pastry. But my partner has disappeared. I was hoping you could help locate her."

"Is it too hot in here, Mr. Continental? You seem to be sweating."

"I'm nervous. There are some papers missing. Important patent papers and trademark forms, regarding the, um, pastry."

"The double decker cupcake?"

Continental gasped. "How did you know?"

"Lucky guess."

"The Cupcake Club is one, but there's another extremely valuable project: Top Cakes. Cupcakes with just the tops. My...associate was suppose to develop my vision."

"And that would be Helen Wolf?"

"Yes!" Continental gasped again. "You know her?"

"Let me ask you a question. Do you know my partner, Archer?"

Continental wiped his brow. "Yes. Yes. He was doing some work for me. He didn't tell you?"

"Refresh my memory."

"I asked him to keep an eye on Ms. Wolf. She was erratic. I wanted to find out if she could be trusted."

Spade started running few database queries on Helen Wolf and her alleged sister, Marie. He looked at Helen's picture, the one he took as she entered his office. She was playing him.

He went out to tell Effie about Archer. She had never liked him. Neither did Ms. Archer, as Spade knew only too well. Neither did Spade, really. He wondered how long Archer had been working jobs on the side, screwing the firm out money. "We'll need a new sign, Effie. No more Spade & Archer. Just Spade Investigations."

Spade finished his database searches. Wolf had no sister. But she did have two kids at P.S. 87 and a husband named Blake. And she had a lease on a test kitchen in near Port Authority. That was Spade's next move.

On the way downtown, took his inventory:

Archer was dead. His beautiful client was a liar. His ugly client seemed like a liar. And kids at school couldn't even buy a goddamn chocolate chip cookie. It was a lousy case.

He suspected he was being played for sap. But what was the angle?

The building that housed Helen Wolf's test kitchen had a back entrance for deliveries. He waited for someone to come out and then went up the rear stairway and jimmied the back door to her kitchen.

He was quiet. But not quiet enough.

Helen Wolf looked up, horrified, and raised the rolling pin over her head.

Spade got in close, too close for her to swing and clock him. He grabbed her wrist and twisted. The rolling pin dropped, and he ripped her arm behind her back and then pushed her against the door of the walk-in freezer.

"What's your game, Ms. Wolf?"

"This is no game. This is war."

"Why'd you lie about having a sister? Why'd you waste my partner? Why'd you sell out Continental?"

"Ask Continental. He's a mole, a front, a fake. He can't tell ganache from red velvet. My people saw him come out of the Department of Education. He was ratting me out."

"Why? What does the D.O.E. need spies for? They're like the Vatican and the IRS. Nobody can mess with them."

"There have to be things more powerful than the D.O.E, Sam. The right to bake for children. A kid's right to cookies. The right to raise funds for trips to Washington, D.C. What are we all supposed to do now? Have another damned book fair? A kid can't eat a book."

"But why'd they take down Archer?"

"I don't know. Ask Continental. I saw them talking outside the school."

Spade spat. Archer. He'd always wondered how his partner seemed to live large on their lousy take. He increased the pressure on her arm. "You saw him last night, didn't you?"

"Yes! Archer crashed our meeting. He knew about our secret bake sale room, an old storage closet by the gym. He tried a Top Cake and a Cupcake Club and told us he believed in our cause. But I saw him slip two of my samples into a bag and I knew he was working with Continental."

"He always had a sweet tooth," Spade said, wondering what the hell his partner had thought he was doing. What ever it was, it sure hadn't worked.

"Could you let go of my arm, please?" Helen Wolf pleaded.

Spade stepped away. He said, "What's Continental's angle in all this?"

"He wants to own my Top Cakes! The same with the Double Decker."

"Didn't he hire you?"

"He was a backer. But these cakes are my weapons against this awful ban. They are so good, so delicious, people will go nuts for them. If we only sell them at the schools, cupcake lovers will take to the streets and force an end to this ridiculous ban. But Continental doesn't care about that. He wants them for Inter-Continental."

"How is it that both of you settled on me? Continental, I get. He was already paying Archer behind my back, but you?"

"The yellow pages."

"The yellow pages died around the same time as Friendster, sweetheart."

"I met Archer once before. He was snooping around the school cafeteria. Your card dropped out of his wallet. I hired you wondering if I could find out anything. Oh, my cupcakes!

I can't let him take my work. Oh, help me, Sam, please!"

"Nothing doing. You're a crummy liar and maybe Continental is, too, for all I know." Spade looked around. His eyes lit on the beautiful woman's desk. There was a big folder on it marked "Top Cakes Project." Wolf leaped at the papers, but Spade was too quick.

"I own these now, sister. You want 'em, tell me what happened to Archer. You offed him, didn't you? And put all the Continental Chocolates there to frame the fat man, is that right?"

"I didn't have a choice!" Wolf cried. "Archer had grabbed my samples. That was all Continental needed to reverse engineer my cupcakes. Then he'd mass market my creation, and destroy the most profitable bake sale in history."

"There's always a choice. I'm choosing to make a phone call." He stabbed a number into his cell and barked the address when Leary answered. "Get down here and bring your cuffs."

Cupcake Killer! screamed the headlines. Effie was spreading the papers across Spade's desk when he came in.

"I can't believe it, Sam."

"Believe it," said Spade, who looked down at Effie and brushed strand of hair off her face.

Effie stepped back. "People killing each other over cupcakes. This town is going to hell," she said, heading to her desk.

"The pizza is still pretty good," Spade called after her.

The door slammed shut. He shrugged, pulled out his iPhone, and punched out a tweet. "Let them eat cake. Case closed."

IN MY TOTALLY NEW CHEECH AND CHONG STONER COMEDY

In my totally new Cheech and Chong stoner comedy, a bequest from the will of Jerry Garcia has been discovered, leaving 1000 acres of primo Colorado farmland to my uncle Cheech Marin and his former pal Tommy Chong, with the stipulation that the two men "must oversee the farming of the land together."

When Uncle Cheech calls me about the will, he totally curses his comedy partner out.

"Whoa," I say, "I thought you guys were okay with working with each other and all that bad mojo from the 80's and 90s was gone."

"It's back. He thinks I sold the golden hookah, man."

"What golden hookah?"

"The one we got when we partied with Shah Junior."

"Shah Junior?"

"Yeah, man. The Shah's kid. It was back in the 70's in a sweet suite at the Plaza. That gold keeps the water cold. I swear, man: You would take a hit and your *cojones* would contract."

"What happened to it?"

"I don't know, man. I thought he had it and he thought I had it. We didn't even remember the thing until like a year ago."

I drop out of college immediately in my totally new Cheech and Chong stoner comedy and fly to L.A.

"Uncle Cheech, you can't just let 1000 acres of primo farmland sit there, barren and weedless. Let's find Chong and grow some power bud. You guys were born for this."

"I don't want to see that guy, man."

"Uncle Cheech, you can buy matching golden hookahs when the money comes rolling in."

"I'm too old to be a farmer."

"I'll farm. You just handle quality control."

"I like the way you think, man."

When Tommy can't be reached by phone, it's time for a road trip because this is a totally new Cheech and Chong stoner comedy. So we drive up to Seattle, our car a mobile cloud of smoke, listening to hip-hop mashups of the Grateful Dead and Santana.

The reason we can't reach Tommy Chong is that he has been working obsessively in Seattle, building the world's largest vaporizer. And just before we arrive, Tommy sends his granddaughter Mila, who is drop-dead gorgeous, out for some vegan ribs. When she's gone, Tommy stuffs a serious bag of weed into the vapo-chamber and tests it. There's lots of hilarious special effects conveying that Tommy has gotten totally wasted—his head rotates 360 degrees, his long hair levitates. But of course Tommy says, "Wow, man. That's an okay buzz, man. I better check the chamber."

Right then, one of Tommy's cats sets off a security

alarm, and Tommy, fearing a bust, or spies, or a rip-off, freaks out, hits his head on the vaporizer and takes off.

When we arrive at the lab in Seattle, Mila is freaking out. Her uncle is missing. The security alarm is roaring. And she's totally suspicious of Uncle Cheech. But I explain the whole Jerry Garcia thing and give an impassioned speech about brotherhood, friendship, America and the manifest destiny of the magical hemp weed, and the role of Cheech and Chong in moving the country in the right direction.

"You are so right!" says Mila. "I tell Grandpa Tommy the exact same thing. They totally took the danger out of weed and replaced it with humor."

"And where would *Harold and Kumar* be without them?" I ask.

"You are so like my twin!" marvels Mila, which is not exactly what I want to hear, but I'll take it.

"Yo, what's this thing?" says Cheech.

"It's Grandpa Tommy's secret project."

"It's like a giant mashpotato-izer, right? A liquefier, blender. A whatchacallit—Cuisinart for pot, right?"

"A vaporizer, Uncle Cheech."

"The world's largest," says Mila. "Grandpa Tommy wants to sell it to clubs and rich clients, so they can have rooms where the vapor is piped in."

"Where is Chong, man?"

"I don't know. I went out to get vegan ribs for lunch and now he's gone. He never leaves."

"He probably heard about the bequest and is just avoiding me," says Uncle Cheech. "I DIDN'T SELL THE GOLDEN BONG, MAN! Come on out and say hello!"

"Does the vaporizer work?" I ask.

Mila goes to the vaporizer and opens the mega-vapo-chamber.

"Oh my God!" she cries.

Tommy Chong's over-sized glasses are lying at the bottom of the chamber.

"I can't believe it!" Mila says

"What?" I say.

"I think grandpa has been…"

"The dude's been vaporized, man!" says Uncle Cheech.

"What do we do?"

"It's Seattle, man. Let's just call Bill Gates or that Amazon guy. Jeff Bozo."

"I don't think it works that way, Uncle Cheech. We need to reverse engineer this."

While I'm on the internet, feverishly trying to find out if you can reconstitute vapor back into its original solid state, Tommy Chong is wandering around Seattle, stoned to the bone, without his glasses.

There are lots of hilarious paranoid moments. Like where a girl offers him a smoothie sample and he thinks it might be poison, so he freaks out and knocks her tray over. In the ensuing panic he walks through a plate glass window and then accidently steps on a pitbull. The dog is vicious and he has to run for it. Fortunately there are two Seattle cops on Segways, and one has stepped off to write a parking ticket. Chong, who is still higher than Mt. Everest, hops on the cop's Segway and takes off, initiating the first-ever pitbull-Segway-Segway chase scene in cinematic history, which is beyond funny because just the word Segway is a hilarious, right?

Segway.

See? Anyway, first the bloodthirsty pitbull gets taken out by a lumbering but perfectly timed stream roller. Then, just when the pursuing cop on the Segway yells, "Stop or I'll fire," someone opens their car door and—boom!—wipes the cop out. Having made his escape, Chong gets off his Segway and discovers he's near his lab.

Inside the lab, Mila is sobbing, I'm trying to search the web and Uncle Cheech is trying out much smaller vaporizers. "These are good. But I prefer the big bamboo, man."

All of a sudden, Chong swoops down on my uncle. "Mila, did you let this bastard in here?"

"Hey, man, back off. I don't wanna have to use my cholo superpowers to kill you, man."

"Grandpa Chong! I thought you were dead!" cries Mila, launching herself at him. "We thought you were vaporized!"

"Yeah, man. Too bad it didn't happen!" gasps Cheech, trying to get out of a headlock.

"Vaporized?" Tommy Chong lets go. "Nah, man. The alarm went off after I did a massive vapo toke and I split."

"Oh! We found your glasses in the vapor chamber," says Mila.

"Why did you let these guys in here, Mila? I told you he's a thief. He stole the Golden Hookah."

"That's B.S., man. You had it. You took it in a taxi to Electric Ladyland, remember?"

"Gentlemen," I say, taking out the legal papers branded with the Grateful Dead's skull and roses insignia, "I think we'll all be in a position to buy our own golden hookahs if you'll just sit and listen."

For the final scene of my totally new Cheech and Chong stoner comedy, there's a huge overhead shot of our amazing farm that races over acres of weed until it comes to our massive warehouse. Inside Mila and I are wearing while lab coats and directing botanists as they test the pH of the soil or whatever it is botanists do. Forklifts carry gigantic bales of primo weed through the building and follow a sign that points to "Quality Control."

Inside Cheech and Chong recline on purple chaise lounges, two giant golden hookahs between them, surrounded by walls of green herb.

"This stuff is pretty good, man," says Cheech. "It has a kick like an elephant."

"Yeah, that's batch 232314 Indo," says a glazed Chong, looking at a clipboard.

"We should call it something else, man," Cheech says, as the camera starts pulling way out in my totally new Cheech and Chong stoner comedy.

"Elephant weed?"

"Sister Mary Elephant Weed."

"That's a pretty good one, Cheech."

"Hey, thank you, bro."

"For a stoned-out, golden-hookah-stealing, klepto-chicano."

"Hey!"

"Just kidding, man."

OFF THE WALL

"They got on well except for the fact that I suddenly got a call from Freddie, saying, 'Miami, dear... You've got to get me out of here. I'm recording with a llama... I've had enough and I want to get out."
—Rock band manager Jim 'Miami' Beach on the collaboration between Freddie Mercury and Michael Jackson in *The Times* of London.

It wasn't just the llama, if you know what I mean.

I was there at the studio. Me: the serf of sonics, the *domestique* of decibels, the peon of pop. Mr. Assistant Engineer. You know—or maybe you don't, since almost nobody records in studios anymore—I was the underpaid, under-washed, under-everything guy who always has a roll of duct tape and walks around connecting wires, hooking up effects, and moving the mic two inches to the left, then one inch to the right, and then tilting it just-so and going back to the control room only to be told by the executive knob twiddler behind the board to go back and "Move it an inch to the right and straighten it up."

Yes, I remember it like I remember all my years as a studio rat: through a nonstop haze of pot and pizza. I was there for practically every second, except when I was sent out on errands to the florist, or to ask Mrs. Jackson to send in some chamomile tea for Michael.

This was all in Encino, at the estate. It was around '83, pre-Bubbles, pre-Neverland, post-*Thriller*. Michael still lived at home. But he had had a state-of-the-art studio installed next door.

We were all expecting magic. Freddie had already spun gold with Bowie on "Under Pressure." Yeah, there were rumors he and Ziggy Stardust had battled over the final mixes. But that's just part of the process. It's not like Freddie was a diva. Listen, you don't get from Zanzibar to Madison Square Garden by lounging on rickshaws eating Indian sweets with weird names like *barfi*. You need to have talent and drive. And I suppose a great mustache helps.

The expectations were huge. Michael had just released *Thriller*. I can remember thinking that I was watching the two greatest musical talents this side of Alan Parsons. That's probably a meaningless comparison to you, but it was my way of saying they were gods, like Skrillex and Danger Mouse are today, right? Or maybe it's DeadMau5 that I mean. I get Danger Mouse and DeadMau5 mixed up.

But that's how good they were. I mean, Freddie had squeezed an entire opera into 5 minutes and 55 seconds, and Michael had worked with Eddie Van Jesus on "Beat It." You don't get better than that.

Anyway, trust me, it wasn't just the llama. It was more to do with the 15-minute discussion Michael had with Mr. Big Shot Engineer about whether the llama was an alpaca or a llama. That time-waster ended with me, the gopher of glam, the houseboy of hip, having to go to Encino library to research the matter. And if that wasn't what irked Freddie, it was probably the next day, when we showed up in the studio and there were four Peruvian pan pipers playing "Human Nature."

"What the hell is this?" said Freddie. "You're not going all Paul Simon on me?"

"Oh no, Freddie," said Michael. "I just thought it might cheer up the llama."

"Good. Because for a minute there, I thought you'd lost it."

"I just love animals, Freddie."

"Is it working?"

"Is what working?"

"Is the llama feeling any better?"

"I'm not sure. Hard to tell. Maybe after the empanadas get here and the vet arrives, we'll know more."

Freddie turned away. Then Michael had the engineer roll back the tape so he could listen to yesterday's vocal tracks for "State of Shock," which Mick Jagger would later sing instead of Freddie. Thinking I would have some time before anyone needed me, the toiler of top forty, the midwife of Motown, I ducked out to smoke a bowl.

Freddie joined me. This happened a lot: Rich rock stars mooching off the roadless roadie. But I didn't mind. This was Freddie Mercury. "Can I have some?" he asked.

"Sure. Is that good for your voice?"

"The llama can sing for me."

"Here." I gave him the pipe and the lighter.

I was thrilled. Usually, I tried not to suck up to rock stars at the studio or ask too many worshipful questions. I couldn't help myself.

"Mr. Mercury."

"Freddie."

"Freddie, this might sound like a stupid fan question, but how did you pick a brilliant punk-before-punk, super glam name like Queen? It's so cool. My band can never decide on a name."

He inhaled and held the smoke. Then he exhaled. "This is good stuff, isn't it? We'll be glad when those empanadas arrive, right?"

I laughed. I was glad someone else thought Michael was a weirdo. But I was a little bummed Freddie ignored my question.

"Listen, I've got to go face the music. But thanks for the buzz."

We both went in. The pan pipers were playing "I'll Be There."

"There you are." Michael was holding a cordless phone and looking at me, the doula of disco, the handmaid of heavy metal, the janitor of jam. "See if you can get a llama specialist from the San Diego Zoo on the phone."

"Yes, sir."

The bell to the studio buzzed. "That must be the empanadas," said Freddie.

"Oh shit!" called Mr. Big Cheese Engineer. "The llama is eating our two-inch tape!"

Michael rushed into the live room where we had stacked some reels, and pulled the animal away. "No, no, no! Bad llama!" he said. Then he started nuzzling the beast's neck.

Freddie turned toward me and reached for the phone. "Actually," he said, "can I borrow this? I just remembered. I have a call to make."

FIVETHOUSANDTWO HUNDREDTWELVE.COM

About five minutes before the opening number of the Academy Awards airs this Sunday, Norbert Kozwinkle will do something that will instantly send the smartphones of Tinseltown bigwigs and grandees buzzing. He will post his projections for the winners of Hollywood's biggest night on his web site, Fivethousandtwohundredtwelve.com.

Mr Kozwinkle has become the oracle of the Oscars thanks to his website, which takes its name from the 5,212 eligible voters for the Academy Awards. Although long a household legend from Hartford to New Haven for his revolutionary actuarial flights of invention, he achieved instant fame after launching his site and stunning Oscarologists with a post that shredded "the Scorsese Effect"—the long-held view that, once alone with their ballot, suave academy members will never vote for short directors with unfashionable hard-shell eye-wear, not even if they happen to make movies like *Goodfellas*, *Raging Bull* and *Taxi Driver*.

"It seemed pretty obvious that there is no Scorsese Effect," says Mr. Kozwinkle from his office at Fealing Mutual on the outskirts of Hartford, where he has worked since graduating college at the age of 18. "Voters have exhibited bad taste and poor judgment before, but there are other factors at work on voter psyche besides a man's glasses and height. And besides, everyone knows someone who has those glasses or is vertically challenged. And many of our heroes—Groucho Marx, Malcolm X, Elvis Costello—have had unstylish spectacles. Heck, I've had them for years, and I'm 5'8", and I was voted Actuary of the Year three times in a row by the National Association of Insurance Professionals. So I knew that America—and even Hollywood—was bigger than that."

Mr. Kozwinkle confirmed his hunch by doing what he always does—studying the available facts and numbers. He looked at all Best Director winners and nominees for the last 81 years. And then he issued his findings in a post on Fivethousandtwohundredtwelve.com. "While I'm still stunned that Mr. Scorsese never won in 1991 for *Goodfellas*—the mind boggles that Kevin Costner won that year for *Dances with Wolves*—Hollywood does not take passes on men who wear glasses," he wrote in that groundbreaking post. "John Ford (4 wins, 5 nominations) wore glasses that looked like those joke-shop nose-and-spectacles combos, Milos Foreman (2 wins, 3 noms) had standard-issue Czech national health numbers, Billy Wilder wore specs, so do Coppola and Spielberg, although the latter's eyewear is generally rooted in the decade in which he is living. Then, in terms of short, bespectacled guys from New York, there's Woody Allen, who won twice with atrocious glasses and bad hair, to boot. Altogether, 33.2345% of Oscar-winning directors have worn glasses."

For those who maintained that in this era of contact lenses, the bespectacled winners were all old timers, Mr. Kozwinkle posted a picture of Steven Soderbergh, who won for *Traffic* in 2001, be-glassesed in a fine pair of chic-nerd frames. Game over.

Well, not exactly over. Mr. Kozwinkle then gave Mr. Scorsese a 92.7% chance of winning, based on his complicated algorithm that factors in genre (dramas have it all over comedies), cast star-wattage, per-screen box office numbers at the time of ballot mailing, number and size of ads in *Variety*, Google search term rankings during that same period, and a myriad of other data. Mr. Scorsese, as the record now shows, did indeed finally win for *The Departed*.

This was no surprise to his colleagues.

"Norbert changed the paradigm," says his boss, Monroe Fealing. "Actuaries told the odds of established scenarios using established data. Norbert pushed to find better metrics—what's the mortality rate in densely populated areas with poor hospital proximity? Guess what? It's pretty high, so we upped our rates. Rainfall by ZIP code was a factor in calculating fatal accidents. It never rains? Great, lower the premium and increase sales. Norbert takes the risk our of risk management and helps us maximize profitability."

"The guy has taken actuarial initiative to a whole new level," says Davis Appleton, columnist for insurance industry bible *Underwriters Weekly*. "He'll never mention it, but he was the first guy to synch New York's Compstat reports with ZIP codes, and turn that information into a goldmine of sales. Fealing started offering unlimited window replacement in areas where smash-and-grab wasn't a problem, and sales went through the roof."

Mr. Kozwinkle's parents, who look a little like Mr. Scorsese, took the Oscar predictions in stride.

"What do you expect from a boy who used to sleep with his abacus?" says his mother, Maureen, an accountant.

"Then I got him one of the first battery operated calculators, and he used to sleep with that," added his father, Andrew, also an accountant.

The precocious, statistically inclined Mr. Kozwinkle never wavered. When other kids were putting up black light posters, the teenaged Mr. Kozwinkle hung a picture of Srinivasa Ramanujan, the great south Indian mathematician on his wall. He declared his majors—Statistics and Algebra—in second grade. How did he veer off to the world of movies and awards? .

"I wanted to do work people outside of the industry could relate to. And I thought, why not analyze the biggest media event of the year and see what I could learn?"

Mr. Kozwinkle is both fascinated and frustrated by the Oscars. "There's not a lot of polling of the electorate— so the data I work with: ticket sales, historical precedent, critical appraisal, other awards—is very work intensive. Then there's the ever-crucial degrees of separation between nominees and voters—you can't underestimate the voting benefits of working with a wide swath of Hollywood."

With Hollywood studios throwing money at him for his research and predictions, why is Kozwinkle holding off on revealing his projected winners until the show is about to begin?

"I did the research. Most people don't want to know the Oscar night results before they are announced. They like the mystery. 83.7402% of viewers, in fact."

MISSING PARAGRAPHS FROM THE N.Y. TIMES' OBIT OF LEROY "SUGARFOOT" BONNER

The great Ohio Players frontman and guitarist LeRoy Bonner died January 26, 2013 at age 69. The following paragraphs were, inexplicably, cut out of the Times obit.

A family member said preliminary tests indicated Mr. Bonner had died from the residual effects of a lifetime addiction to funk.

"They said they had never seen a man with such a pronounced case of funk. It was everywhere. His clothes, his heart. All his major organs were covered in funk, just like the vocals, horn charts, and guitar riffs of the Players' songs. Not to mention the album covers. Those covers were 100% funk."

A source in the medical examiner's office noted that most of Mr. Bonner's funkiest work was recorded before the music video era, a fact that probably added years to his life.

"Look, if the band had made videos for 'Fire' or 'Honey' or 'Love Rollercoster,' it would have exposed Bonner and his band to dangerously high levels of funk. Remember, this was 25 years before internet porn. The average human couldn't cope with that kind of funkiness back in the day."

Symbolist poetry scholar Bernard Le Pretense noted that funk did not just consume the band's sound and looks, but also their lyrics. "Just look at the opening lines of 'Fire,'" Le Pretense said, pinching his nose and declaiming:

> *Hey, now, huh-huh*
> *Hey, hey, hey, no, (Ow, now)*
> *Hey, now, huh-huh*
> *Hey, hey, hey, no*

"As you can hear, it is really a cri-de-coeur for more and more funk," Le Pretense explained.

Dr. David Stock of the CDC, and an avid record ("well, CD") collector, expressed mild surprise at the longevity of funkateers. "Frankly I'm a little surprised we haven't seen more funk-related deaths. But I suppose the Eagles and Air Supply really cut down on airplay back in the 70's. Which ruined radio but saved a lot of lives."

THE BROOKLYN INVITATIONAL NOBEL PRIZE FOR LITERATURE FANTASY LEAGUE DRAFT

It's the second round of 2014 Brooklyn Invitational Nobel Prize for Literature Fantasy League Draft at Commissioner Dave Carpenter's apartment in Sunset Park, and Margaret Atwood and Joyce Carol Oates are still on the board when it's my turn to pick.

My team, The Stockholm Syndrome, is going heavy on women this year. The ladies are overdue. Sure, Artisanal Artie Weggle's Ghostface Poets won with Alice Munro last year. But before that, it had been four years since the Academy had picked a woman, Herta Müller, which pissed off the entire league because nobody had ever heard of her, never mind drafted her. All of which is to say, I crunched the numbers and the Nobel bigwigs have *a lot* of catching up to do in the women department.

My first-round pick, Algerian novelist Assia Djebar, provoked a huge amount of derision for being a pretentious pick. *Wanker, wanker, wanker,* went the chant at the table. But I feel really good about Djebar. She's got tremendous upside: Totally obscure, woman, Muslim. I was set to take French playwright-novelist Yasmina Reza in the second round, but the Commish got her with the last pick of the first round, which detonated a *Too Young, Too Young, Too Young* chant that I happily joined.

So there they are: Oates and Atwood, two masters with all the tools. My pre-draft power rankings have Oates at #15 and Atwood at #13. Neck and neck, really. Of course, I don't always follow my power rankings, which factor in pure talent, contribution to literature, and whether I think an author deserves to win. Philip Roth is ranked #1 for the sixth straight year on my list. But after years of picking him, I've learned my lesson. If he's still on the board in the fifth and final round, I'll take him, but only because true love dies hard.

I put down my power rankings list and flip through my scouting report. *Joyce Carol Oates: American. Writes to all fields: novels, poetry, drama, short stories, YA. Ontario Review. Oprah factor. Rumors of HGH use tied to prolific output, probably bogus.*

Then there is this: *Margaret Atwood: Quadruple threat, novels, criticism, nonfiction, activism. Doyenne of Dystopia. PEN. Spunky grandma everyone wants. Canadian like Munro.*

Do the other teams know something I don't? You would think these women would be on everyone's top 20 list and off the board by now.

Phil-ip-Roth! Phil-ip-Roth! Phil-ip-Roth!

Then I remember. They are playing hunches, too. Louise "Princess Kale" Mayfield is doing what she always does with The Bushwick Bookies: hoping the Academy picks an African or black American. She nabbed Ngugi wa

Thiong'o (down to #27 on my power rankings) with the third pick, and made Percival Everett (up to #16 on my P.R.) her second round choice.

Max "Remember Dial Up?" Beier, owner of the PoMoMoFos, is picking South American authors. Again. Dial Up used the PoMoMoFos' first pick on Eduardo Halfon, a Guatemalan Jew who has a book—a good one—called *The Polish Boxer*. But really, the guy isn't even 50. And Sergey "Google Gogol" Gomes is convinced that Arabia is bound to carry the day. His team, The My Back Pages, has picked the same guy for three years running: Adonis. ("You know," says the Commish. "The Charles Atlas of Arab poetry!")

There is one minute left on the clock (you only get three minutes, per league rules). A new chorus starts in an attempt to distract me: *De-Lil-lo! De-Lil-lo! De-Lil-lo!* At least it has a nice meter.

I'm thinking hard about the Academy. They go for a body of work. But what does that mean? Do they want Oates, whose body is sort of a gothic-tinged literary octopus with ADHD, or Atwood, who is known for her novels and essays, but is really just as varied and versatile as Oates? I close my eyes and think: *The Handmaid's Tale* or *We Were the Mulvaneys*? *The Blind Assassin* or *them*?

The chant has changed. One side of the table says *Julian Barnes!* And the other responds: *Ian McEwan!*

"Okay, shut up!" I say, standing up at the table. "The Stockholm Syndrome proudly deploys its second-round pick to select Margaret Atwood."

Instantly the chant switches to *Too Canadian, eh! Too Canadian, eh!*

"Atwood's like, vice president of PEN, too." I say,

defending my pick.

Nancy "No-Name" Walker, who used her first pick to select Pynchon—I mean, an American man in the first round? *Has she learned nothing?*—immediately stands up. "After a deep interior monologue," she says, "Walker's Home For Lapsed Recovering Novelists emphatically select Joyce Carol Oates!"

Steroids! Steroids! Steroids, goes the chant. No-Name turns to me. "You know, Owen, I was going to take Atwood..." she says.

"Really?"

"...in the sixth round."

Jhumpa! Jhumpa! Jhumpa!

It's a cutthroat league.

YOUR NEW FALL LINEUP

Acknowledging that the crop of new television programs last year was almost a complete washout, the networks are spending big this year to promise, if not genuine excitement, at least something different.

—*NY Times*, May 15, 2011

Memo: Save Your Season
To: All Desperate Network Honchos
From: Andy Drenzi, ADHD Entertainment

Guys, last season didn't work out so well, did it? We're here to help.

Listed below are our projects in development to save your upcoming seasons. We have incredible focus group testimonials and a social marketing plan that is more infectious than anything the CDC has ever encountered. But really, as you know, the show is the thing. Along with the script and the cast and a strong lead-in. And a huge marketing budget, too. But you gotta have the right show.

Extreme Hold 'em: Poker games are much more exciting in Westerns. Why? Guns, alcohol and women. In this series, cards talk, but so do fists, knives and guns. Gives new meaning to calling a bluff.

Ironman Chef: Cooking with a freaking staff? Where's the drama in that? Two chefs, one wedding, no help, 12 hours. Attendees vote on the food.

Pimp My Pimp: Real youth market potential. Street wear companies are very excited by this edgy show, co-hosted by Divine Brown and Ashley Dupré. Women request total makeovers for their boyfriends. Public outcry over the title is guaranteed. But so what? Our testing shows no one cares!

Dancing with the Stars with Real Actual Stars: I know. Genius, right? So long, Chaz Bono.

Project Run-Away: Street urchins form street teams, each shepherded by a pillar of society (Linsday Lohan, Khloé Kardashian, Donald Trump) to promote things of true importance: mixtapes, liquor, athletic footwear, deodorant and cellphones. Each episode the most creative teams win and stay on while members of the worst team get kicked to the curb.

Shotgun Weddings: Young women recall that blissful night of conception, complete with blurry, soft-focus dramatizations of back seat quickies, basement debasement and prom night naughtiness. Then they recount those tense and tender moments, 6 to 20 weeks later, when their beloved baby daddies get the news. Filled with ballistic mothers, furious mother-in-laws, monosyllabic men, and dozens of "will they or won't they" moments, each show is a wild ride on the way to the whipping—I mean, hitching—post.

I'm enclosing a link so you can see the pilots, which all tested through the roof. Yeah, I know your shows all tested through the roof last spring. And the spring before that. But we raised the roof a little higher this time. Trust me.

The bidding starts Wednesday at 3 pm Eastern, 2 pm Central and 12 pm Pacific.

Best,
Andy

THE AVERAGE JOE'S GUIDE TO POETRY TECHNIQUES AND MEETING WOMEN

"What did he do to you?"
"He looked at me and told me metaphors."

—*The Postman*

The most common question Average Joes ask us during our Poetry Seminars (call 1-800-AVERAGE)—not including, "do you really serve beer during class?"—is this: "So what is a poem, anyway?"

Good question.

There's a lot of confusion about what makes a poem a poem. Does it have to rhyme? Does it have to sound purple and pretty? Do you have to use all those stupid things like symbolism and metaphor and meter? Does it have to have a certain amount of lines or syllables? Does it have to sound best in a poncy English accent?

Poetry is a wide-open format. Imagine you are so rich that nothing matters. On April Fool's Day you can send Warren Buffett a check for his grandchildren's college fund. When war breaks out in far-away lands, you can actually buy peace by offering warring factions staggeringly large sums of money. You can throw big parties and invite lots of famous, beautiful actresses and rock stars and All Star basketball players, and then send out "You're Not Invited" cards to the people you hate. You can hire personal trainers to help you lose your Average Joe beer belly and then take supermodels on elegant dates to islands with two-syllable names like Fiji or Bali.

Okay, now wipe that silly grin off your face. Good. That sense of freedom you just had—the idea that you could do anything—is the same idea behind writing poetry. You can say anything you want to say, any way you want to say it.

Just break up sentences in funny ways and never use paragraphs.

There are other elements that make a poem a poem, too. These are called poetic techniques. They can be crucial to your development as a poet and as a ladies' man—so pay careful attention.

RHYME

Depending on who you ask—and yes, we know we should have said "whom you ask," but we are just Average Joes here—there are either lots of schools of poetry or only two. The people who say there are lots of schools of poetry are usually scholars. They know about things like pastoralism, the romantic movement, the symbolists, the modernists, confessionalists, the beats, whatever. The people who say there are only two groups of poetry are us.

There's poetry that rhymes and there's poetry that doesn't.

In general, we prefer the rhyming kind. For one thing, rhyme has a ring to it. Some rhymes are perfect, like hat and cat or Marilyn and drinking gin. Other rhymes don't quite cut it. They're broken or forced, with a similar-but-not-quite-right sound. These, however, can also be very effective. Like, say, Pamela and Wonderbra.

Rhyming is sometimes sneered at in certain uptight, over-intellectual circles. This has to do with the stigma of nursery rhymes, which some people assume are for merely children. Of course, nothing could be further from the truth. A lot of nursery rhymes are terrifying—look what Jack got for going up the hill with Jill: a fractured skull. And many, like those of the great and wonderful Dr. Seuss, are deeply philosophical. The Sneetches, for instance, tackles social inequality, while The Lorax reads like a green party manifesto.

But the anti-rhymers do have a point. Some poems are better off not rhyming. These are poems about solemn issues. It is not, for example, always a good idea to rhyme a poem about death. Or about a painful divorce or about failing to cover on the Super Bowl. Some things should be treated with respect.

Here's a poem that gets to the heart of a subject that is very painful to most Average Joes. Clearly rhyming is not needed.

HEATWAVE
Don't touch me,
don't even look at me.

It's much too hot
for the horizontal mambo.
—Nanette DeNono

Here is another. This is a very painful poem that any Average Joe can instantly relate to:

LOVEBURN
The pain in my heart now
matches
the stinging sensation
I experienced
elsewhere
on my body
this morning.
—Gustave Crank

ALLITERATION

This is a device that is similar to rhyming. Despite being a big word, it's a simple idea. When a few words in a row begin with the same sound, then—bing, bang, boom— that's alliteration.

Here is one of the lesser works of Verlaine de Tookey, which will surely elucidate how to alliterate.

THE CONCUBIND
Sexy Suzy Sundays
Merry Mary Mondays
Tasty Tammy Tuesdays
Wacky Wendy Wednesdays.
Toothsome Thelma Thursdays
Freaky Frida Fridays
And Sweet Sandi Saturdays
When will I do my laundry?

A word to the wise: too much of anything is too much in general. And too much alliteration sucks and is really annoying. If you constantly use this device, you are going to bum your readers out. And that, of course, is something you don't want to do. Remember—and we can't stress this enough—most of the people who read poetry are women.

FLOWERY LANGUAGE

Flowery language can be a real pain. It sounds nice and impressive, but Average Joes sometimes get a headache listening to poesy. "What's the point?" we find ourselves asking. "Why don't poets just talk in plain English?"

Before we go any further, we must tell you a story. Once, a former student of ours, an Average Joe, just like you or me, went out with a girl. She was a very cultured, liberated, intellectual Italian-American babe. They went back to the old country one summer. On the plane ride back home, his girlfriend wanted to know what his favorite image of the trip was.

Our former student thought a minute. He weighed going with the Sistine Chapel, or the trip to Florence, or the endless shoe shopping he was forced to endure. Then he shared the truth. "You know," he said, "I really thought all those girls riding bikes were really hot. I wish they did that back in New York."

Wrong answer, bambino! She broke up with him the minute they passed customs. He was too blunt. It was only after attending a second seminar with us that he realized the power of poesy.

A few years later, this same guy went back to Italy with a different woman, one who was just as cultured, but who tolerated Average Joes a little better. He sat at cafés and discreetly enjoyed the lovely, leggy thrill of pedaling señoritas, all the while composing a poem in the softest of words. And when his girl asked him to name his favorite thing about Italy, he was armed with some very flowery language.

ITALIA

Of all sight's sweet caresses
none can rival
girls on bikes
in dresses.

His girlfriend laughed and gave him a big kiss. So flowery language has its good uses.

Of course, the ultimate tale of the power of flowery language exists in the story of Cyrano de Bergerac. Here was a guy who could control the intoxicating power of beautiful words. Cyrano understood that flattery could get you nearly everywhere and helped his tongue-tied friend seduce a smoking babe named Roxanne. Tragically, however, the friend died before he could close the deal, if you know what we mean. Leaving Cyrano, who was also in love with Roxanne, to agonize over the whole thing. What's the moral of this story? When your friend is dead, he's dead. And if you happen to be in love with the woman you helped him woo, then step up to the plate and tell her.

SIMILES AND METAPHORS

A simile is like a metaphor only different.

A metaphor is a simile without the like.

What does any of that mean? Basically, a simile is a poetry technique writers use to compare two dissimilar things using the words "like" or "as."

Here's an example of a very famous simile from a very famous poem:

> VENUS IN DENIM
> Stacked like a library,
> the girl with the biggest hair
> walks by wearing acid wash jeans
> that could only have been
> painted on
> with a very fine brush.
> I think I love her.
> —Tony Beltnotch

See? The author, the incomparable Beltnotch, is comparing a girl to a library—which is to say the girl is, er, intelligently put together. See how effective this choice of words is? He could have said, "Stacked like Kim Kardashian," but that would have cheapened the image. Plus, what is more stacked than a library? Absolutely nothing, that's what, since libraries have stacks and stacks of books. Clearly, by using one perfectly placed simile, the reader knows Beltnotch is talking about the ultimate woman.

Metaphors are a trickier animal. Writers sometimes use them to compare things (just like similes). But they also use them as stand-ins or symbols. Think about every argument you've ever had in your life. "It's apples and oranges." That's a metaphor. Think about watching baseball and how a pitcher "throws smoke." Think about football and the huge lineman who "is a monster." Think about that wild girl you knew in college who was "an escaped mental patient in bed." See? You already know how to rock the house with metaphors.

Here's a poem that is a direct and obvious metaphor:

UNSELFIE-ISH
Love is not an iPhone 6
but my old Galaxy Note 4
with your picture
on the home screen.
—Ernesto Amici

Okay, let's go over this in slo-mo. The whole poem works by comparing two phones to describe love. Amici sets this up beautifully. First he dismisses any thought of love being a new, trendy, overly expensive phone like the iPhone 6. Then he contrasts the slick sizzle of that phone by mentioning the enduring allure of his huge-screened, lower-priced Galaxy 4 Note. But he doesn't stop there. He then personalizes his feelings, declaring it is not just the smart phone that defines love, but the image of his beloved on his home screen that does the trick. Really, this is a tremendous use of metaphor. One that anyone can instantly understand.

Now a lot of Average Joes ask us about symbolism and metaphors and similes and say they can't think of any. "I'm not poetic enough," they say, whining like little kids. As people in old novels say, that's just stuff and nonsense.

A guy once came to us swearing he couldn't write a single line of poetry. He was so desperate we decided to help him free of charge. "What do you feel like?" we asked.

"What do I feel like?" he repeated, looking at the can of Pabst that we provide each Average Joe at every seminar. Then he thought for a minute and smiled. "Say, that gives me an idea," he said, grabbing a pen. This is the poem he dashed off:

OFF THE WAGON
Here's a simile that inspires cheers:
Every day I feel like a couple of beers.

"Gee, that was simple," he said, after we congratulated him on a fine poem. "I am such a dumbbell!"
"Nice metaphor," we said.

MICK'S WORK OUT REGIME

As Mick's personal trainer, I get asked a lot of questions. Why would he ever get out of his super-model encrusted bed to spend time with me at dawn? Does he use collagen? What drugs is he on? Does a 70-something rock star still get groupies? What the hell was Keith doing in that tree? The truth is, Mick isn't just a world class singer and a world class sex symbol, he's world class athlete and a world class businessman. He's just world class. He knows that time waits for no one, so he puts it all on the line. Plus, if you're going to charge people outrageous sums of money for tickets at huge stadiums, you better be in damn good shape to deliver a hell of a show. And that's where I come it. I've put together a little primer on how Mick says "Start Me Up" every morning—and builds muscle for his signature stage moves.

Before They Make Me Run Warmups—Ha, ha. That's a Keith song. My little joke. Hey, rock stars need to warm up like anybody else. We do the basic stretches, we steal some stuff from yoga, pilates, yogilates, gyrotonics, gyroyogilates, tai chi, chilatesyogyro, qigong, aqua-aerobics, and of course, gryoaerobicyogilates. You should pick and choose, too. It's only rock and roll. Once we're warmed up—usually in about 20 minutes—we get down to the good stuff.

The Jumpin' Jack Flash—This is essential to for any rock frontman. You think clapping your hands overhead is easy with 60,000 watts of light pouring down on you?

1. Go into a sauna
2. Turn strobe light on
3. Perform one jumping jack with a resounding hand-clap at the top of the jump
4. Alternate with a one-leg high-kick and overhead clap
5. Repeat sequence 10 times, switching high-kick legs, then get the hell out of the sauna. Don't forget to turn off the strobe.

The Nagging Hand Of Fate—Wild gesticulations—like the conniptions of an irate, spasmodic schoolmarm—can be very dangerous. In Geneva, Mick actually dislocated his pointer with a finger wag. You can see the pain streak across his face on YouTube during "She's So Cold," but he's such a competitor—nobody can endure pain like Mick can, his threshold is unreal—he finished the set and ordered me to reset his finger on the spot. Painkillers? Nothing more than a bottle of Evian. Lately, Mick has eschewed the hand flap in favor of the safer point-at-the-crowd, but you never know when he might bust one out, so we build up hand strength this way:

1. Call security and make sure there are no unauthorized video cameras on the premises.

2. Crank Village People's "Macho Man" on the stereo,

3. Lift two five-pound weights in front of you, until your elbows are parallel to your shoulders, palms facing outward.

4. Flex your wrists down and up in time to every vocal phrase that comes on the downbeat

5. Do this for the entire song. To vary the routine, do the same moves to "YMCA," but integrate the weight flexes with the YMCA dance.

The Jacket Flail—The wind can be treacherous at these stadium shows, and one zipper or button in the eye can end the whole tour. So that moment when Mick takes off his jacket and waves it over his head is one of the most dangerous moves of the evening. We work to make sure Mick has totally great arm strength. Warning: You'll need a lot of space to practice.

1. Take one jacket with zipper pockets and fill with sand

2. Put on jacket

3. While running, strip off jacket and grip the center of the collar (this ensures the jacket will be balanced)

4. Lift hand straight overhead, bend elbow slightly

5. Rotate arm and wrist in small circles that grow bigger by the fourth circle

6. End the fifth rotation by flinging the jacket outward. Repeat steps 2-6 5 times.

These next two sequences are designed to improve Mick's unique funky chicken moves, which I have always thought of as...

The Red Rooster Strut

1. 5 backwards shoulder rolls
2. Lock core, puff out chest
3. Flex and raise elbows
4. Pound elbows against rib cage 3 times

After 10 reps, add the following steps for the...

Squawk Walk

1. Prance 5 steps to the right
2. Prance 5 to the left
3. Extend right hand in front of you and point
4. While running forward, add 3 mild thrusts forward
5. Return to pounding elbows against the chest.

Repeat 5 times

Lip Curls—who needs collagen when you have this secret weapon?

1. Pull lips tightly together and slightly inward, as if you are trying not to react to a stupid remark like, "Bon Jovi is just as good as The Stones."

2. Now slowly extend your lips outward. Stretch until you can actually see your upper lip.

3. Feel the burn? Hold for 5 counts.

Repeat 10 times.

This is the perfect warm up for an exercise that, as far as I know, only Mick and Angelina Jolie can execute.

Lip Ups—That's right. One-handed pushups are for weight-lifting wimps.

1. Wrap your lips around your teeth
2. Lie flat, hands behind your back, mouth to the floor.
3. Inhale through your nose and lock your core.
4. Unfurl your lips, pushing your head, neck and body upward.

3 reps of 5.

Then we run. Or rather, Mick runs. I watch.

SUBMISSIONS EDITOR AT DREAMS QUARTERLY

Dear Mr. Smith,

A dream in which you "do something nasty with a family member"—and particularly a "distant cousin," which, frankly, we hear about all the time—in no way merits inclusion in our magazine, no matter how arousing you may have found it.

Please see the Frequently Recorded Dreams page on our website to determine whether your dream is worthy of submission.

Sincerely,

Donald Wembly

Submissions Editor

Dreams Quarterly

American Academy of Dreams

Dear Mr. Smith,

Thank you for submitting your "unique nocturnal reverie," as you call it, to Dreams Quarterly.

While dreaming that your mother was performing spot-on impressions of Judi Dench is indeed an original detail as yet unregistered in our database, the rest of your dream—falling from a huge edifice that might be the Empire State Building or maybe a castle but you "can't be sure"—is the kind of murky, pro-forma submission we get all the time, and it does not pass muster with our panel of peer reviewers. And yes, we had a hunch that you would wake up before you hit the ground.

We thank you for thinking of us and wish you well placing your dream elsewhere.

Donald Wembly
Submissions Editor
Dreams Quarterly
American Academy of Dreams

Dear Mr. Smith,

The opening of your dream was riveting to many of us. No one in the office could recall a dream about being transformed into a duckbilled platypus in any of the literature, although some older members remember a rash of Howard the Duck appearances in the seventies. A search of our database confirmed the unique quality of the dream. Sadly, however, many of us lost interest when you started screaming, "It's me! It's me!" and no one could hear you. We heard you, and we cannot offer you a place our magazine for such a cliché development. But we will enter it into our database, and encourage you to try again.

Your dreams are showing steady improvement.

Donald Wembly
Submissions Editor

Dreams Quarterly
American Academy of Dreams

Dear Mr. Smith,

So, so close! We very much enjoyed the image of you performing "Singin' in the Rain" amid a downpour of Skittles. Frankly, there is a disappointing lack of candy in most submissions. That this happened during your big presentation at work and in front of the boss you hate, however, is something with which we are very familiar, as is the jump cut to you having sex with your junior high school French teacher while conjugating the verb "conjugate."

I myself had that exact dream when I was fifteen, except her name was Madame Prefontaine, not Madame Vega.

Again, perhaps it would help if you performed a keyword search in our Dream Index to see just how common your dreams are before submitting them. I must say, though, that you have mastered the opening sequence. Now, if you can just keep that inventiveness going a little longer, and avoid the common plot points and fogginess that afflict so many dreams, you will really have something.

All the best,
Donald Wembly
Submissions Editor
Dreams Quarterly
American Academy of Dreams

Dear Mr. Smith!

I am thrilled to tell you that no one in the recorded history of dreams has ever transformed into a "thought leader."

This innovative, groundbreaking, trendsetting, pioneering term for being an innovator, a creator, a trendsetter, and a pioneer brought much laughter to the office, and we can't thank you enough. We got a little worried when you told your parents that you were, in fact, a thought leader and they didn't understand. But then when you addressed a barn full of baaing sheep dressed in business suits with sheep-drool-covered smartphones in their mouths, it was simply a sublime moment of resentment transference. The finale, where all the sheep are bleating, "It's me! It's me!" and you say, "Who cares? I'm a thought leader, goddam it!" and then a pack of sheepdogs bursts in to herd them away while you deliver a lushly diabolical laugh, was thoroughly cinematic. And we loved how you morphed a common identity trope into a revengeful power trip. Really first-rate.

So it gives me great pleasure to write that you have now achieved the stuff dreams are made of—inclusion in our next issue. Congratulations!

We await your next submission, you thought leader, you.

Don

IN MY IMMATURE GUY GETS STUCK WITH LITTLE KIDS COMEDY

In my immature guy gets stuck with little kids comedy, I've just finished college with a double major in botany and partying, and I cap off graduation week by winning the New York State Beer Pong Championship, because even though I'm a weedster, I also speak fluent brewski.

And at this, the most triumphant moment of my life, my girlfriend tells me she's dumping me because I "really need to grow up."

The next day I have a DEFCON 1 red alert hangover. After I wake and bake, and then quaff a hangover cure of Pepsi, raw egg, Tabasco Sauce and mint chocolate chip ice cream, I drag my sorry ass home.

As soon as my parents see me, they both start screaming: "A botany degree! You just want to grow pot!" which is true. And then, because my parents do everything together, they have matching heart attacks.

They survive, of course, because they have to tell me that their day care center, which has been in the family for

150 years, is going to be condemned. "Please, save it," they whisper in near-death voices.

The next morning I open up our Kids Space day care center. It's a nightmare. I meet a cute girl with Tourette's syndrome and the vocabulary of a sailor; a kid leaking snot; a girl with a thick head of hair who asks me to check her for lice; and a boy who really needs something but stutters and coughs so badly I can't understand what.

Meanwhile, I'm studying the walls, looking for a chart, a schedule, anything that will help me understand the flow of the day. I can't ask any parents in my immature guy gets stuck with little kids comedy, because, obviously, I have to act mature.

Inside the classroom, a future criminal is trying to glue a turtle onto a fire truck, while his future cellmates are throwing blocks at each other. And I'm frozen, wondering what to deal with first when suddenly I hear a bunch of handclaps.

All the kids stop what they are doing and answer with five handclaps back.

"What in the world are you guys doing?"

In the doorway of the classroom is a vision. For some guys the perfect woman comes from the land of Pornistan: teased hair, big boobs that don't really move that much, high heels, pouty, rouged mouth. That's not this perfect woman, even though I have no problems, really, with the Pornistani perfect woman. No, this perfect woman has curly, messy reddish-brown hair, green eyes, a warm smile, small boobs and is wearing a thrift shop dress with sneakers.

"Georgie, put that turtle back in the cage. Robbie and Taj, the blocks are closed. Lawrence, do you need your asthma inhaler? Here. Now I see we have a new guest in the room. Do I know you?"

This vision is smiling at me.

"I'm Reed. Reed Taylor."

"Reed? Vanessa's son?"

"Yes," I say, moving closer and lowering my voice "Mom and Dad are in the hospital."

"Oh, no. That's awful."

"And you are?"

"Lizzie. Lizzie Murphy. I'm the teacher."

So I spend the next few weeks trying to impress the hell out of Lizzie Murphy, which means smiling when the kids fill a plate with glue and get me to sit in it. Or laughing when they tape a "kick me" sign to my back and hammer at my shins.

What Lizzie doesn't laugh about is a letter from the city. We have one month to raise $100,000 and get the building up to code, and pay off property taxes. Otherwise, the city will condemn it, seize it and sell it.

"Oh, Reed, that's awful. We have to have a fundraising appeal."

So an email goes out and we raise $5,000. It's not enough, but it gives me an idea.

I call my botany buddies up at school and I check on our little "indoor garden project." The news is good and when the kids have been picked up, I invite Lizzie to dinner. She can't go; she has her sign language class and then has a shift at the homeless shelter at a local church. "But I'd love to another time. Really!"

"How about tomorrow? Then I can tell you my plan for Children's Space Cakes."

"What?" she says.

"We are going to make space cakes—brownies in the form of a rocket ship."

"But our bake sale only barely make any money."

"These are going to be special. $100 an order." I said, looking her in the eye.

"Oh," she says. "It's not just about the rocket ship, is it?"

"Exactly."

The rest of my immature guy gets stuck with little kids comedy moves really fast.

A smarmy real estate guy comes tour the grounds with his diva girlfriend, and the kids get him good with the glue on the plate trick, which ruins his $2,000 suit. They also sneak an oozing, runny slug into the diva's Coach handbag, which detonates a screaming fit and an early exit.

I explain my fundraising operation to a few select moms and dads who are in a dire need of a hookup and have no connections. I make 500 real space cakes and 500 faux, unenhanced ones that are just rocket shaped cakes. They both cost $100, though, which is worth it because we use vanilla icing to coat the rocket, and chocolate to do the graphics: USA, NASA, NORML.

At the $100,000 Children's Space Cake Emergency Fundraiser, a cop shows up, which is a major bummer. But he is so offended by the $100 price tag, that he stomps out and goes to Dunkin' Donuts.

Later, we're down to the last Rocket Cake, when the cop comes back with some buddies. "Hey," he says, picking it up. "We were talking. This cake must be pretty special."

Lizzie looks at me in horror. But I stay cool and take

the money, even though my heart is in my throat.

But instead of bagging the evidence, cops each take a bite, and then another bite, until they eat all the evidence, which really saves the day.

The last scene in my immature guy gets stuck with little kids comedy is the Pre-K graduation ceremony. The little kids all bust funky dance moves when Lizzie and I hand them their diplomas.

And then Lizzie and I bust some moves of our own, and when we kiss, all the kids shriek and freak out and yell "cooties!"

Then some supremely funky Nile Rogers guitar cranks up on the soundtrack and the credits roll.

FREEZE DANCING
WITH THE STARS

Dear PTA Members of Rollins Elementary,

Just a quick note of thanks to everyone who helped out at Saturday's historic event!

Our first ever Freeze Dancing with the Stars Jamboree! was an exciting, music-and-movement-filled day of juice boxes, bake sales and face painting, and, most important, raising money for our afterschool program.

But there were a few issues that surfaced and I'd like to talk about them now.

Let me start with the poster for the event. *All* Rollins Elementary staffers are stars! Not just Ms. Kamen, Mrs. Ellis, Mr. Bolacky, Ms. Downey, Mr. Gluck, Mrs. Rodriguez and Principal Davis. But there was only so much room on the poster. I apologize if anyone felt left out.

I have just come from visiting Principal Davis in the hospital. He would appreciate it very much if the teachers who felt slighted over the poster would withdraw the grievance filed with the union.

Leading by example, Principal Davis will not pursue a legal case against fourth graders Tommy Lucas and Dennis Lavell for pouring soapy water on the dance floor while he was doing the electric slide.

Seeing Principal Davis being taken out of the cafeteria, immobilized on a stretcher, was a frightening sight for all of us. But watching all 42 girls in the fifth grade deliver a twerkfest before the entire school—I'm talking Miley Cyrus drinking Red Bull spiked with Spanish Fly—was also a little disturbing, if not more so.

On Monday, therapists will be on hand to help any traumatized students, like my second grader Marie, who witnessed the vibrating mass of overly made-up tongue-flashers before I could cover her eyes.

We are still trying to find out how Robin Thicke's "Blurred Lines" was substituted in place of the Jackson Five's "ABC." Fifth grader Jordan Appleby, who made the pre-approved mix, is only talking questions submitted through his attorney.

The sight of some dads, as well as a certain gym teacher, video taping our twerking fifth graders was also distressing.

On a positive note, it was a delight to see so many kids, parents and teachers enjoying themselves the first hour of open dance floor.

Unfortunately, when the freeze dancing competition started, some children had trouble following the rules. Thankfully Assistant Principal Morris, her megaphone and threats of detention proved invaluable at keeping the competition moving.

We are all also very grateful—with the possible exception of the still incarcerated Doris Grumman, the mom of third grade twins Monica and Melissa, and Donald Fort, the injured father of kindergartener Fredric—that our security guards

Mr. Thomas and Mr. Honeywell were on hand to enforce the dance floor decorum for some of our older contestants.

I'm happy to report that we reviewed the videotape of the competition, and Ms. Grumman's violent, pizza tossing assault on our judges was totally unjustified; she was clearly late in freezing in round of 15,

As for top ten finalist Mr. Fort, he was indeed caught moving mid-pivot when DJ Science Teacher froze the floor during Bruno Mars' "Treasure." Looking at it in super-slo-mo, his right foot keeps moving for a nanosecond more than the other dancers.

The glass display case in the lobby, which showcases our annual Good Citizen award and which Mr. Fort shattered on his way out, has been repaired.

Here's hoping the severed tendons in Mr. Fort's right hand can be fixed just as quickly!

Since so many contestants left after being eliminated from the dance floor and missed our final Freeze-Off, allow me to congratulate our three winners. First grader Tammy Vorster in the K-2 division, fourth grader Darryl Stone in the 3-5 division and Mr. Gluck in the adult division.

I am proud to say we raised $1638.50!

Our next event is just around the corner. If you'd like to compete in "Project Funway," the entry fee is $20 per team. You can also order tickets to the event's finale, a 5 pm fashion show/judging competition. I am really looking forward to an event that celebrates creativity and teamwork. Get your needles and scissors ready for what should be a truly wonderful, drama-free event!

Delores Brown
Chairwoman, Fundraising
Rollins Elementary PTA

PRE-ARRANGED RITUALISTIC INTERPERSONAL CONTACT

My Dear Professor Ludwig,

Our study, *The Ramifications of Pre-Arranged Ritualistic Interpersonal Contact Among North American Non-Married Cohorts,* is nearly complete. I feel more confident than ever that we have incontrovertible statistics that will shine the academic klieg light, if you'll pardon the expression, on the causality of consummation.

I have been feeding the data into our extremely virile algorithms, and as you can see in the attached document, no matter what the coefficient is, the results are astounding! Whether a walk in park, a Big Mac at the mall, a cup of coffee, a movie, or even a day at the museum followed by Indian food at a Bangladeshi-owned restaurant and a long subway ride home, almost any formalized interaction of two people of compatible sexual orientation between the ages of 18 and 35 and of similar attractiveness, increases the likelihood of sexual activity by 10,000%.

With such arousing numbers, it seems pretty clear that

two mild-mannered social anthropologists with frighteningly huge computational powers—namely you and I—are destined to become famous. Perhaps our prowess will lead to some much-needed respect from our peers, although I use that term lightly. I can tell you that I certainly wouldn't mind some Pre-Arranged Ritualized Interpersonal Contact with Dr. Penelope Leakey-Horowitz. And I'll never forget your witticism about one day going on "an excavation" with Dr. Anastasia Toledo. Outrageous comedy, that. As you'll see in the data, it appears that intimate sexual coupling of some sort, be it "necking," "snogging," "canoodling," or "making out" (30%) or the more graphic "getting to second base," "fondling," "heavy petting" or "oral stimulation" (30%) or the full on, close-the-deal coitus of "going all the way" or "doing the horizontal mambo" (40%) happens after 2.6 sessions of Pre-Determined Ritualized Interpersonal Contact (PDRIC) sessions.

Factoring in sessions in which more than two alcoholic drinks were consumed, such intimate bonding behavior happens after an astounding 1.3 PDRIC sessions among subjects younger than 28. If they are 28 or older, alcohol induced bonding requires 2.2 sessions.

Clearly, alcohol is a coefficient that will have to be studied further.

When the subjects engaged in normal, non-pre-arranged everyday activity, most interactions, be they work lunches, shared commutes, or pre-school drop offs, did not lead to anything more risqué than a couple of Advil or a glass of wine before 5 pm.

The control group that went out in groups of three or more had no physically intimate relations during our monitoring period, either. It appears that three or more people going out on the town interferes with sexual activity for some reason. A reduction of pheromones, maybe? Who knows? Interestingly, our second control group—the married couples we sought at the last minute—revealed that the likelihood of sexual relations within 24 hours of PDRIC did not rise, no matter how much alcohol was consumed. Perhaps this is an outlier? I have my doubts about including it in our study.

I urgently await your feedback. Also, do you think the title is too balanced for such a bombshell report? I don't want to bury the lede, as they used to say in movies about newspapers when there used to be newspapers. The alternative title I've been playing around with is not entirely academic sounding, but here goes:

Does Dating Lead to Sex?

Let me know your thoughts.

Proudly,
Dr Milton Godowsky

THE MCKINSEY REPORT

"It was more about an initiative I have going on with both teams that I hired McKinsey & Company [a Manhattan-based global management consulting firm] for, because as I've gotten to look at both our organizations, it's become apparent that we really need to reprocess both teams."

—James Dolan, owner of the NY Knicks
& NY Rangers in a *NY Post* interview

Our marriage wasn't really thriving the way I thought it should. So I called McKinsey Consulting to see if they could help Jane and me.

They sent over a well-scrubbed young man wearing an expensive-looking suit. "Harris Decker," he said, offering me a big smile and a firm handshake.

"Thanks for coming. Should I go get Jane?"

"No, no, no. I'm your account representative, Mr. Handler. I'm just here to give you an overview, get the paperwork started and make sure we have the right team in place to give you the results you need."

"Great," I said.

"Exactly! So what we do is we like to learn about your relationship. What the issues are. Short-term goals? Long-term goals? Deal breakers? Is there any low-hanging fruit we can address immediately for a quick win?"

"Excuse me?"

"You know, are you or your wife having a affair? Do you talk when your mouth is full of food? Does your wife talk to your cat like it's a three-month-old baby? Does she spend tons of cash buying things from web sites you've never heard of? Things like that, which, if identified early, can have an immediate impact."

"No. None of those."

"Don't worry, we'll find some. We'll also be comp-ing you against best of breed couples to see where you fit on the marital spectrum."

"I don't really care about other couples. I care about me and Jane."

"Well, it's always helpful to know the industry standards so you can establish a baseline. That way we can figure out what an acceptable ROI is for each of you.

"ROI?"

"Return on investment. What are you giving and what are you getting? Also, is the supply chain, you know, for your emotional and physical needs, breaking down? If so, when and where does the breakdown occur? Are you following me?"

"I think so," I lied.

"Great! We rely heavily on metrics. So tomorrow, when Ravi and Pete get here, they will do a deep dive into your numbers."

"Our numbers?"

"You know: sex, duration of, frequency of, initiator averages, perceived satisfaction index, actual partner satisfaction index, segmented by category with accompanying graphs. Plus, your ACL and your IFR."

"What are those?"

"Average Conversation Length and Income-to-Fornication Ratio."

"Oh."

"And then, of course, they will fill out the ultra-important Spousal Satisfaction Survey with each of you."

"Is that it?"

"If you have the budget we can set up video feeds in the kitchen and living room and dining room. "

"But isn't the bedroom where the problems arise?"

"Not as much as you might think. Our research shows your pre-pajama interaction determines what happens behind the bedroom door."

"Interesting."

"Exactly! Then our personal branding expert will review the tapes and work with both of you to improve your brand with each other."

"My brand? I'm a person!"

"To you, you are person, no question. But to other people—especially those closest to you, and don't take this personally—you are a collection of tics, quirks, bad jokes, questionable hygiene and stock responses. That's you, the product."

"How can I not take that personally?"

"Sorry. We try to work on how you can inspire positive associations with the product of you. We want to maximize your positives and remove the negatives and make you the most attractive brand, if you will, that you can be."

"How much is this going to cost?"

"We strive to work within your budget."

"Suppose my budget was very small?"

"We advise a minimum $20,000 engagement."

"20 grand?"

"That is a good deal cheaper than a divorce, Mr. Handler."

He had a point. "Okay, then at that end of the 20 grand what happens?"

"We give you a report with a topline dashboard, supporting analytics based on other use-cases and best of breed couples, followed by our recommendations and a list of best practices."

"For both of us?"

"Oh, yes. It's very comprehensive.

"And the implementation?'"

"Implementation would be another engagement, with our project management division who are pros at helping you hit your markers."

"Okay," I said lamely. "I'll think about that."

"Great. So I've prepared a contract. Here's a hard copy but there's also one in your email. You can red-line the document and just email it back. Okay? Great. Any other questions?"

"Just two," I said. "Are you married?"

"Me? Are you kidding? I'm 23 and single. *With a job!* What's the other question?"

"Do you mind explaining all this to Jane?"

SEGWAY IN OVERDRIVE

You know how there are these internet music discovery applications like Shazam that—when you hear a tune and you don't know the title—can tell you the name of the song and the name of the artist who recorded it? All the app needs is a snippet of the music. It converts the snippet into a set of data points, sifts through a database of millions of songs and their respective data points, and finds the perfect match in, like, nanoseconds. I have it on my iPhone. Anyway, soon—I'm guessing 5 years—you're going to be able to do that with pictures. How awesome would that be? Say you see a hot girl. You take her picture, feed it into this new app and—boom!—you find out her name is, like, Yolanda Friedberg. Whoa. And then you can Facebook her, friend her, email, and maybe hook up and even fall in love. It's coming. It's a no-brainer. Everyone's facial features and dimensions are different. Eye shape, nose length and width. Flared nostrils, lips, philtrum, which is that two sided-groove between your nose and upper lip. Sure, the coloring and photo quality and angles will make it tough to figure it out. But with the computing power and search programming going on these days, it's a sure thing. Take my word for it, I'm an engineer at TechnoGogo.

I was thinking about this because I saw an amazing-looking girl today on the subway. I looked up from my iPhone—I had been playing with that old Theremin app that makes eerie, woo-woo sounds when you wave the phone around—and I immediately stopped what I was doing. You know how when someone catches you playing air guitar while you are hooked into your iPod, and you feel like a total jerk? That's how I felt using the Theremin app, but worse. But as I checked out Superbabe 5.0, I realized she was reading a book and probably hadn't seen me acting like a moron. Anyway, as this 3D-designer I know at work says, her graphical interface was exceptional. I thought about taking her picture just to have for that day in the future when I could use it to look her up. But I was transfixed. She had reddish brown hair, which might have been dyed or hennaed, in a pseudo bob with bangs (or is that redundant? I guess a bob always has bangs, right?). The angular cut framed her fine, high-cheekboned face. Her skin was olivesque, if that's a word, like she might have been Indian or South American, and all of that fit together in this perfect, symmetrical, crystalline beauty, but that wasn't the best part.

The best part was she had freckles on her cheeks. I'm not talking pale-skin with pox-like-freckles. I'm talking two, sexy clusters of off-brown, slightly reddish pixels. Mysterious, subtle dots that somehow reminded me of a leopard. Something wild, exotic and beautiful. To borrow a phrase from another guy I know at work, those freckles on this face totally put my Segway in overdrive.

I did some analytics. She was sitting down, but I could

see she was tall, about 5'8". Maybe 23 or even 25. No rings on her fingers. She had a bag on the floor between her feet, and when the train lurched, she bent down to steady the bag and I could see part of her lower back and I was really relieved that she didn't have a tattoo, which normally I don't mind on a primal hookup level, but it is a little trashy, right? That's why some people call it a trampstamp. Do women think men are going forget to look at their butts unless they have one of these? No, we're not. So that tat—I call it a backtoo—is like an unnecessary icon over your rump that says "click me."

Really, we don't need any encouragement.

Anyway, even though she was elegant enough to get away with some Chinese characters or some kind of spiritual sign, like an om, on her lower back and make it seem classy, I was glad there was no backtoo. She was already perfect. And that is what I was thinking when we pulled into West 4th Street and she grabbed her bag and got off and so did I because, man, she was it. And I thought I was risking never seeing this girl again, even with all the power of TechnoGogo behind me—not to mention Google and LinkedIn—because I didn't have her name or where she worked or studied or lived. Nothing.

So I got off the subway behind her, which I suppose is creepy and stalkerish, but what could I do? She had long legs that looked longer than they actually were because of these elegant, thin leather boots that fit over black jeans that hugged her like some kind of second skin.

I followed her toward Washington Square, and this other girl bumped into me. At first, I thought she was what one of the guys at work calls "a 20-foot-blonde"—at 20 feet away you are very interested; at 4 feet, not so much. But she smiled at me and I smiled back. And she was actually a lot cuter than a 20-footer, but, well, have you seen the original Kindle? If the Kindle were the first hand-held device on the planet you might have thought it was cool. But in the age of the iPod, the Blackberry, and other gadgets which were like Orgasmatrons you couldn't let go of, that first Kindle just looked completely dorky. I wouldn't even touch it when it came out. It was like, digital cooties, man. Anyway, it's the same thing with the girl who bumped into me. In different circumstances I might have been interested, but not now.

We were almost to the park and I'm thinking, what next? I did some quick calculations: Me: 5'10", 32, fit, jeans, Billabong sweatshirt, blond, lanky slacker hair. Her: Helen of Troy. I didn't need my PhD in programming to know that the chances were slim to infinitesimal that she would find me as intriguing as I found her. But the sun was shining. It was a beautiful fall day. And sometimes the wisdom of crowds and the laws of probability are wrong. Sometimes the site you want isn't at the top of the first page of search results; sometimes it's at the bottom of the tenth page.

"Excuse me, Miss?" I called to her.

She stopped and gave me an uncertain, questioning look.

"I know this is weird, but I saw you on the train and…" I was blowing it. I was dying. "I don't usually do this. I, um, I work at TechnoGogo."

Kill me now, right? I forged ahead:

"Do you know what a cascading search is? It's a term used when a system queries a series of databases. In a nanosecond, it goes from table to table of data looking to answer the query. Shopping sites use it to find the product you are looking for and tell you what is in stock and what's not. Well, life is like that, too. We all run non-digitized cascading searches. You know, we search to find apartments, friends, jobs, pairs of shoes. We just go on and on, looking. But when I saw you, I felt like, wow, I want to meet you. My name is Derek."

"Nice to meet you." She had a low voice. I love women with low voices.

Then she stuck out her hand for a shake. What can I tell you about shaking hands with a beautiful woman that you don't already know? It's pathetic, like walking into a presentation with an ancient laptop and having to ask for USB, because your machine can't handle wireless.

"My name is Hope."

"Derek," I said again, like a moron. "Derek Miles. Engineer. TechnoGogo. I live near Wall Street."

"Look," she said. "I have to get to class. How about you give me your email and we can connect."

"Great," I said, "My email address is Derek Miles at TechnoGogo dot com. That would be awesome. I can write it—"

"I gotta run, derekmilesatTechnoGogodotcom. Nice meeting you!"

I watched her walk away, fast and tall and glorious, her reddish-but-brown hair shining in the sunlight. I wondered what class she was going to: Grad school, yoga, medical school? I should have noticed the title of the book she was reading. Then I thought about her name. It was so earnest. Part of me liked it, part of me wanted to like it, and part of me wondered who the hell names a child Hope? Religious people, hippies, people with nothing. But maybe people who are just good normal people, too, who like the sound and the meaning of a name. I wondered if the U.S. Census bureau collects first names. It would be interesting to see the socio-economic backgrounds of people with names that mean something overt in English: Hope, Chastity, Desire, Prudence. How about Logic? Or Trust? Anyone give their kids names like that?

I got to work and checked my email. No Hope. I knew that. I expected that. I replayed our meeting scene in my head and I reached an inescapable conclusion: It was earnest, but there wasn't that instant impact, that connection. I did not make the same impression on her as she had made on me. I was bummed.

I thought about her boots. What is the story with boots? They are like a slightly more calculated version of the backtoo. I mean, boots send a message and the message is somewhere between Lara Croft and Catwoman and Venus-in-Furs. Right? Or maybe it's about being chic, plain and simple.

Hope really threw me for a loop.

Just around lunchtime, at 12:14 p.m.—email is so precise, isn't it?—a message from ImHope2001@hotmail. com hit my inbox.

To be totally honest, this is how I reacted:

1. Yes!

2. Hotmail? WTF?

I couldn't believe she emailed before lunch; based on my lame introduction, I figured she'd play it cool and email this evening or tomorrow. Then I tried to remember the last time I got an email from a hotmail account. I searched my inbox. 2010, January.

Hope2001's e-mail told me I was sweet. It also said that she was going to do fieldwork about marriage dowries in India next month. Then she asked me what book, movie and CD (as if I would actually listen to a CD! I haven't bought one of those things in, like, eight years) I'd most recently liked.

I read her email two more times, trying to decode it for deeper meanings, for even a tiny glimmer that she was interested in me. Then I decided to chill and not think about it. I walked across the building to the east bank of elevators to go to the company cafeteria on the fifth floor. Then I waited. For one of the most efficient companies in the world, these elevators are an embarrassment. But honestly, it's TechnoGogo's fault: we have offices on eight floors and so too many people use the damn elevators to go from 8 to 4 or 6 to 8 or 7 to 3. So naturally, this intra-floor travel increases everybody's waiting time for elevators, because elevators aren't optimized for intra-floor travel. They are built to get you from point A to point B and back, the first floor being point A.

I finally made it to the fifth floor and had some organically raised but obviously inorganically killed chicken curry over organically grown yams (I know this because there are signs telling me where all the food comes from). And I started wondering if I should invite Hope to lunch here to enjoy the opulent spoils of corporate life, or whether she'd care. With a name like Hope and fieldwork in India, there's a chance she'd be annoyed by this whole place. But then I saw Melissa, who is an account rep, making her way from the food disposal rack all the way toward me. She is a 3-foot blonde, which means she has a big, broad, super-warm smile and a great bod, and you are interested at any distance. And just watching her made me smile. She took the empty seat across from me, asked about the project on I was working on. Then she mentioned that there was a cocktail party after work on the 4th floor, and that I should come.

Before she left she reached across the table and patted and squeezed my forearm, which was like morse-code to the body: dot-dot-dash. Translation: please come drink tonight.

That put me in a good mood. At the elevators I met Steve Choi, who is a funny guy.

"What's up, man? How's your future ex-wife?"

"Funny you should ask. I just got an email from a really beautiful girl. A heart stopper."

"Excellent."

An elevator arrived. Small miracle. We got in.

"But it was from a Hotmail account."

"Oh! I know, right?"

"Yeah," I said.

"It's pretty hard to take someone seriously if they're still using, like, Hotmail or AOL."

At my desk I Googled Melissa and found out she went to college with my best friend's sister and that she used to do theater. I found some pictures of her in a production of *Chicago*, and concluded that if I had gone to that school at that time, Melissa probably would not have had much interest my nerdy collegiate incarnation. But here she was now, making time for me.

Toward the end of the day, I read Hope's email again. I gave it another close inspection. It was devoid of flirting. It was facts and questions. The only ambiguity was the word "sweet," but given the context, it wasn't really that ambiguous.

I tried to picture her face. That mesmerizing sprinkle of freckles on her brown skin was fading under the pressure of eight hours of elapsed time. I should have taken her picture with my iPhone instead of playing with the stupid theremin app. Then I remembered: *Hotmail. Leaving for India.* What was I thinking?

I hit reply and wrote that I really liked *Programming in Objective-C*, *Watchmen*, and the vinyl LP of Animal Collective's *Merriweather Post Pavillion,* which I had just bought used at Other Music and ripped so I could listen to it on my iPhone.

I wanted to write something else. But it seemed pointless. *Hotmail. Hope. Leaving for India. Out of my league. No Hope.* I read her email for a fourth time. There was nothing there. Not even close. To her, I was probably a 20-foot dude. I started typing again.

"You know this morning? I apologize for it, or, at least for my babble about searches. I got it wrong. A good cascading search has logic to it. It rifles through a pre-established hierarchy of tables driven by a set of rules and launched by a query. This morning my query parameters weren't defined. I hadn't even had coffee. Now that I think about it, it was reckless, unfocused. It was completely delusional searching, inspired by an accidental result, not by an informed query or even a random query. I hope that makes sense. And so I wish you, my accidental result, all the best. Have a great time in India. Derek."

I hit send. Then I backed up my work files for the day and headed to the elevators to look for Melissa.

Thanks to:

Michael Agger, Emma Allen, Daniel Blackman, Kevin McLaughlin, Daniel Menaker, Leigh Montville, Susan Morrison, and Bill Tipper.

Eliza Kirby for editing.

Sarah Masterson Hally for designing.

Theo, Hilary, and, of course, Susan, my chief allies in the war.

SETH KAUFMAN grew up in Manhattan and spent his high school years in Nairobi, Kenya and New Delhi, India. A recovering journalist, his work has appeared in dozens of publications. His novel *The King of Pain* was called "One of 2012's most enjoyable novels" by the *New York Times*. He lives in Brooklyn with his wife and two children.